The Acts of God

THE
ACTS
OF
GOD

by
George Sweeting

and
Donald W. Sweeting

MOODY PRESS
CHICAGO

Moody Press, a ministry of the Moody Bible Institute, is designed for education, evangelization, and edification. If we may assist you in knowing more about Christ and the Christian life, please write us without obligation: Moody Press, c/o MLM, Chicago, Illinois 60610.

Library of Congress Cataloging in Publication Data

Sweeting, George, 1924-
    The Acts of God.

    Bibliography: p.
    1. Bible. N.T. Acts—Meditations. 2. Church—
Biblical teaching—Meditations. I. Sweeting, Donald W.
II. Title.
BS2625.4.S83   1986   226'.606   86-16375
ISBN 0-8024-0497-9 (pbk.)

2 3 4 5 6 7 Printing/LC/Year 91 90 89 88 87

Printed in the United States of America

Contents

Introduction

In a technological society, life moves in the fast lane. We live in the middle of an explosion of information, an economy of growth, a revolution in high technology. Many live at jet speed and often find it difficult to cope.

By striving to be people of action, some have lost a grip on who we are and why we are here. As members of the Christian church, we are not exempt from this. The time has come for a checkup. The book of Acts tells of a people of action who knew exactly who they were. They were not only doers, but they slowed down enough to see God's perspective and to listen to His voice.

That potent combination of listening and obeying resulted in the most dynamic and important institution the world has ever known—the appealing, spontaneous, irresistible New Testament church.

There is no better exercise for a local church than to study the acts of God in the first century. The New Testament book of Acts is the ideal place to begin.

It is our prayer that you will measure your life and the life of your church by the pattern presented here. Luke's history is a blueprint, though it is not an exhaustive one. It tells of the basic structure and leaves the rest to the unique creativity of each team who builds and to the Holy Spirit who guides.

Study this structure. Examine the foundational principles. Master them, and apply them.

We earnestly pray that these studies, originally written for radio broadcasts, will aid you in that exciting task.

Acts 1
The Acts of God's Power

> The great difference between present-day Christianity and
> that of which we read in these letters is that to us it is pri-
> marily a performance, to them it was a real experience. . . .
> To these men it is quite plainly the invasion of their lives by a
> new quality of life altogether. They do not hesitate to de-
> scribe this as Christ "living in" them.
>
> —J. B. Phillips

For real estate insurance companies, the phrase *act of God* is
reserved for times of unpredictable, unpreventable destruction in the natural world. It describes the freak occurrences of
nature—earthquakes, floods, hurricanes, or tornados. Those acts
of God are rare occurrences, the timing and occasion of which
defy human explanation. They are so unpredictable that insurance companies place them in a category requiring special cov-
erage.

Much like modern science, insurance companies find
themselves needing a "God of the gaps." That is especially so for
areas that cannot be analyzed as a human accident or a rational
misjudgment. It is surprising to hear such a phrase in a society
that has almost succeeded in banning God-talk. Only the unexpected disappointments cause us to draw on the language of
theology, and even then it is a profane borrowing.

But according to one professional, a doctor of the ancient
world who also happened to be an evangelist-historian, acts of
God were anything but freak occurrences of nature.

That author is Luke, who gave us the third gospel and the book of Acts. The gospel of Luke is an account of the life of Jesus. The Acts of the Apostles is a record of the original church and the acts of God. We could just as well call it "The Acts of God in Bringing Forth His Church," for something powerful took place that transformed and multiplied the followers of Jesus. A combustible faith was ignited, and its flames swept like a prairie fire through the Mediterranean world.

What was it that changed that small band of discouraged disciples into courageous ambassadors of Christ? The answer is one great act of God made up of many acts of God's power. Those acts of power were the daily experience of the followers of Jesus. What evidence do we find of that power in the first chapter of Acts?

THE LORD OF POWER

Front and center in Acts 1 is Jesus, the Lord of power. His place is dominant in the entire book. When Luke talks about the church, he is talking about Jesus. At times in church history that order has been reversed, and the church has become an end in itself. But Luke knew that the church could go nowhere unless Jesus Himself went before it.

That is why Luke's correspondence to Theophilus began with the gospel. It told him about "all that Jesus began to do and teach" (Acts 1:1). That was the only preface possible for such an account.

To Luke, Jesus was the Lord of power. He was almighty God dwelling among men, who had power over life, death, and the future.

The Lord of power was Lord over life. That is implicit in the first three verses. God had visited men. In the first chapter of Luke, an angel tells Mary that the "holy offspring shall be called the Son of God" (Luke 1:35). Does that sound impossible, that God could become a man? It did to prominent Greek philosophers of the day. They held that God was too remote to come in contact with a fallen material world. But Luke records in that same chapter that nothing is impossible for God. God can surprise the philosophers and take on man's humanity. But more startling, God can take on human suffering as well. He can know firsthand the weaknesses of our flesh as He did in Jesus, the Lord of power who dwelt among us.

But the Lord of power was also Lord over death. Verse 3 speaks of the "suffering" of Jesus. That word really encompasses all the suffering of death. Triumphantly Luke tells us that Jesus "presented Himself alive . . . by many convincing proofs."

Luke tells his friend Theophilus that there is an incredible new fact of history that must be reckoned with. That fact is that Jesus arose from the dead. It is a fact that disturbs the skeptics.

Frank Morison, a respected British lawyer, believed that the resurrection of Jesus was a myth. He began writing a book on the last days of Jesus' life, ignoring the miraculous. But after carefully studying the facts from the viewpoint of a lawyer, Morison changed his mind. He laid forth in his book *Who Moved the Stone* the powerful evidence that Jesus did rise from the dead.

It was the resurrection of Jesus that brought hope to a desperate world. It is the resurrection of Jesus that has made knowing God a possibility. The gloom and despair of the crucifixion has been dispelled and a new way opened to us by the Lord of power.

But most important, the Lord of power by His resurrection and ascension (vv. 10-11) demonstrated lordship over the future. Here we find the basis for Christian hope. Not hope in this present world or in the accomplishments of man but hope based in our all-powerful Lord.

There is nothing here of industrial development. There is no mention of technological achievement. Not a word of human progress or self-improvement. The hope is found solely and simply in Jesus' blueprint for the future. In verse 3, Luke tells us that Jesus spoke about the future kingdom. In verse 11 he explains that the Lord of power will come back again. The angels said, "Why do you stand looking into the sky? This Jesus . . . will come in just the same way as you have watched Him go into heaven."

Some will remember General Douglas MacArthur's departure from the Philippines during World War II. Dramatically

MacArthur promised, "I shall return." Three-and-a-half years later he kept his promise and freed that country from Japanese control.

The promise of the Bible is, "This Jesus . . . will come in just the same way as you have watched Him go into heaven" (v. 11).

THE PROMISE OF POWER

What other evidence of God's power do we find in Acts 1? We see not only the Lord of power but also a promise of power.

Jesus promises power to His followers in verse 8: "But you shall receive power when the Holy Spirit has come upon you; and you shall be My witnesses both in Jerusalem, and in all Judea and Samaria, and even to the remotest part of the earth."

According to verses 6 and 7, the disciples were confused. They thought that after displaying God's power through the resurrection, Jesus would now use that power to take His rightful place as king. They ask in verse 6, "Lord, is it at this time You are restoring the kingdom of Israel?" Jesus answered, "It is not for you to know times or epochs which the Father has fixed by His own authority" (v. 7). What they were to know, however, was that they would receive power to witness to the world about Jesus Christ.

The disciples expected Jesus to restore the kingdom instantaneously. But Jesus told them of another plan. They were not to know God's timetable. Furthermore, they themselves were to have a part in God's plan as witnesses. They would be equipped for that assignment by the power of the Holy Spirit. They were called to do something they could never accomplish in their own power.

The engine of a prop plane will do the aircraft no good by itself. The explosive power of fuel must be introduced and a propeller added. Then the engine can pull the craft through the air causing it to lift off the ground.

In Acts 1, the Lord of power extends His resurrection power. It is the only means to accomplish His plan. It is the gasoline of obedience and the propeller of witness. Without it, the Christian life is nothing but a sputter and a cough of false starts. Without it, proclaiming the gospel to the ancient world would never have got off the ground. The disciples desperately needed divine power—and so do we today. A. C. Dixon used to say, "When we rely on organization, we get what organization can do. When we rely on education, we get what education can do. When we rely on eloquence, we get what eloquence can do. But when we rely on the Holy Spirit, we get what God can do."

THE PATH OF POWER

Given the promise of power, what then is the path to God's power? The answer is *prayer*. Prayer in Acts 1 is a cry for God's help. In verse 4 the disciples are instructed to wait. They prayed as they waited. Verse 14 tells us, "These all with one mind were continually devoting themselves to prayer."

Obedience and prayer go together. Do you wonder why Peter stands up in verse 15 after praying and starts the selection process for a new apostle? The Holy Spirit guided him through prayerful reading of the Scriptures. He was shown that there must be twelve apostles for the task at hand. Notice the order of the events. Continual devotion to prayer came first—along with a saturation in the Scriptures—and then came the activity that God desired for His people.

What about your church? What of your life? Do you make plans on your own and then offer up a few quick prayers asking God to bless? For the most part those are not plans born of the Holy Spirit.

Our first business as believers is to give ourselves to prayer. Prayer should be an attitude, a conversation that runs through the day. Paul said that we are to "pray without ceasing" (1 Thessalonians 5:17). And that is exactly the path to power that produced the earth-shaking activity of the apostolic church.

Once Charles Haddon Spurgeon was showing some visitors his church building. After visiting the large impressive auditorium he said, "Come, and I will show you the heating apparatus." Expecting to see a dusty old room containing a broken-down furnace or possibly some clean, recently installed unit, his guests were surprised when he took them to a room where more than four hundred members were kneeling in prayer. The power of the church came from the prayers of God's people. It always has, and it always will.

THE PERSONS OF POWER

If prayer is the path of God's power, then who are the people of power? They are those who have been transformed by Jesus, quickened by the Holy Spirit, and given to prayer. Those are people of power.

For the most part, the disciples were ordinary men. The raw materials God uses are not usually the impressive metals of the world. Jesus called fishermen to be His ambassadors. And if God could use them, then there is hope for you and me.

The three who were closest to Jesus—Peter, James, and John—were fisherman—common stock, hard working, earthy, sometimes carnal and impetuous. Yet God enjoyed entrusting His gospel to them. What became of that motley lot of twelve? For Christ's sake they became evangelists and martyrs. People marveled that men with no formal training could be eloquent and powerful in the preaching of the good news.

Although the Bible is silent on all but the martyrdom of James, tradition informs us of the activity of those common men. Peter went to Rome and was ultimately crucified upside down. John preached in Asia Minor and suffered persecution. James died by the sword of Herod Agrippa. Andrew probably went to Greece and Philip to Phrygia. Thomas visited Persia or India and is said to have died from a spear. There is evidence that Bartholomew preached in India and was flayed alive for his testimony. Matthew may have gone to Ethiopia, Persia, or Pontus. James the son of Alphaeus is said to have preached in Jerusalem; tradition suggests that he was clubbed to death. Simon the Zealot probably went to Egypt, where he was martyred. Judas, the son of James, probably went to Persia and was killed there. Traditions surrounding Matthias point to a ministry in Judea, Cappadocia, or Ethiopia. Those are only the testimonies of the twelve apostles understood by church tradition. Besides them, we know of many other Christians who were killed for their bold witness,

Stephen being a prime example.

What motivated common men to go to the ends of the ancient world and serve Christ? It was supernatural power given to them by the Lord Jesus through the Holy Spirit. God became active in their lives.

What about you? Have you said yes to the Lord of power? Have you received His Spirit of power? Do you walk along the path of power and talk with God about your own call as a witness?

Now is the time to make a new start. Open your life to the power of God and let Him act in and through you this very day.

Remember

Listening to God and obeying resulted in the world's most dynamic institution—the New Testament church.

Through the resurrection and ascension Jesus demonstrated supernatural power available for the future.

The Lord of power promised to share His power with each believer.

Prayer and obedience produced the promised power in the lives of ordinary people.

Questions

1. What impact does the resurrection have on our witness today?
2. What is the relationship between Scripture reading, prayer, and obedience?
3. Look at your life and personality, and compare them to those of the disciples. How were they transformed into what they became? How can you tap that power?
4. How can you translate into your everyday life the concept that prayer is an attitude?

Assignment

Make a list of Old Testament characters who experienced a change by God's power.

Acts 2
The Feast That Never Ended

It is impossible for that man to despair who remembers that
his helper is omnipotent.

—Jeremy Taylor

An American pastor standing near the base of Niagara Falls
exclaimed to a British minister, "Here is the greatest unused
power in the world!"

"Not so," replied the minister. "The greatest unused power
in the world is the Holy Spirit of the living God."

Acts 2 records the events surrounding the coming of the
Holy Spirit. This chapter dramatically and graphically tells us
what happened when the Holy Spirit came upon the followers
of Jesus.

We have a tendency to forget that the power displayed at
Pentecost is the same power available to us today. But instead of
feasting on the Holy Spirit, we starve without the awareness of
His presence and power.

Even though Pentecost took place many centuries ago, its
spirit is alive today. Pentecost is a feast that never ended.

"What does this mean?" (v. 12). The visitors to Jerusalem
asked that question as they observed the Christians on the Day of
Pentecost. As you read about the "rushing wind" and the "tongues as of fire" in Acts 2, perhaps you ask, "What does this
mean?" In this chapter, we see the Holy Spirit moving with mystery and might.

Pentecost was one of the feasts of Israel celebrating the

blessing of God's presence. In Old Testament times, Pentecost had two meanings. First, it was a celebration of harvest. Israel took time to thank God for His faithfulness as Provider. They gave Him the firstfruits of the harvest.

Second, it was a celebration of deliverance. It was a redeemed people—delivered out of Egypt—who gave thanks. The celebration included a sin offering and a peace offering to reaffirm the need for deliverance.

In intertestamental times, a third meaning was added to Pentecost. The feast was regarded as the celebration of a covenant between God and Israel, remembering the giving of the law on Mount Sinai.

Around A.D. 30, when the events of Acts 2 took place, the celebration of Pentecost included those meanings. Yet the Christians added a further interpretation. They saw Pentecost in the light of the Lord Jesus and the Holy Spirit of God. For believers in Jesus Christ, this feast was a celebration of a *new harvest* in the gathering of Christ's church. It celebrated a *new deliverance* based upon the resurrection of Jesus. And Pentecost celebrated a *new covenant* under which Gentiles and Jews became equal in Jesus Christ.

Christians saw that something new was taking place in God's dealings with mankind. The tongues of Acts 2, wherein each man heard the gospel in his own language, stood for the beginning of a new unity. It reversed the conditions resulting from the Tower of Babel. A common language began spreading to different nationalities and races. It was the language of salvation born of the Holy Spirit.

When someone gives a large party or feast, at least three essential facts must be published. Each of those is found in Acts 2. First, the occasion of the feast must be proclaimed. The occasion tells us a lot about the spirit of the event. What kind of feast is it? Is it joyful and glad or mournful and sad?

Second, the host of the feast: who is giving the party? That gives us a clue as to what we should expect of the event.

Third, the guests at the feast: who is invited? The party cannot be crashed; only those with an invitation may attend. But if the host is rich, you can be sure the menu will be more than adequate.

THE OCCASION OF THE FEAST

Acts 2:1-21 discusses the occasion of the feast. For those 120 believers who had assembled together, the feast served as the church's birthday celebration. As the spirit of life shows itself in the conception of a baby, so the Spirit of God manifested Himself in the birth of the infant church.

What kind of a birth was it? It was a birth characterized by the old themes of Pentecost, redesigned by the Holy Spirit.

As the old Pentecost spoke of harvest, deliverance, and covenant, so did the new Pentecost. The occasion of the feast marked an exciting *new harvest*. In the Old Testament salvation belonged to Israel. By living in the covenant, Israel was to become a light to the nations. But because of disobedience, the light failed to go forth as the prophets visualized. With Jesus Christ and the birth of His church, God's salvation now would be carried into all the world. It reaped a harvest for Jew and Gentile, a mind-boggling, brand-new harvest.

The church's birthday also marked a *new deliverance*. The new deliverance began with the resurrection and ascension of Jesus. It climaxed with the coming of the Holy Spirit. That Spirit, whom Jesus plainly promised, would do the Lord's work among the Lord's people. He would call men to an exodus from sin and death by means of a cross. He would lead those who followed into the promised land of resurrection life. He would bring joy into the hearts of the people. At the church's birthday men were not filled with wine, but they were intoxicated by the person of the Holy Spirit.

Along with a new harvest and a new deliverance, the occasion of the birthday also meant a New Covenant. The Old Covenant existed between God and Israel. It was mediated by the priests of the Temple and proscribed by a written law. But the New Covenant would be between Christ and His own from every nation. Jesus Christ would be both priest and offering. The New Covenant would be written not on stone but on the hearts of men and women by the Holy Spirit.

The occasion of the Pentecost feast was a birthday—the birthday of the church.

THE HOST OF THE FEAST

Parties and feasts do not just happen—they are planned and announced. In ancient times, the king or the lord of a household sponsored the banquet.

Who was the honored person on the Day of Pentecost? Verses 2:2-39 provide the answer. It was none other than Jesus of Nazareth, the one "attested to you by God" (v. 22) as "Lord and Christ" (v. 36). Peter announced the Host's name in verses 22-24:

> Men of Israel, listen to these words: Jesus the Nazarene, a man attested to you by God with miracles and wonders and signs which God performed through Him in your midst . . . this Man, delivered up by the predetermined plan and foreknowledge of God, you nailed to a cross by the hands of godless men and put Him to death. And God raised Him up again, putting an end to the agony of death, since it was impossible for Him to be held in its power.

What kind of Lord was He? Following the themes of Pentecost, we see Jesus as the *Lord of the harvest*. His right to that title received its confirmation by His resurrection.

Like a seed, Jesus died, was buried, and then rose in newness of life. Elsewhere Jesus is called a "firstfruit" of salvation. He is qualified to be our Savior. He is qualified to gather a people together. And He calls us to follow His pattern. He calls us to die and rise as He did—as a way of life.

Jesus was also the *Lord of deliverance*. Though crucified, death could not hold Him. For that reason, Paul triumphantly exclaims in 1 Corinthians 15:55: "O death, where is your victory? O death, where is your sting?"

The same power that delivered Jesus is available to the people of God today.

Jesus may also be rightly called the *Lord of the covenant*. The Host of the great feast not only gathers and delivers His guests: He makes a promise to them. God, in Christ, promises to send the Holy Spirit and then pours out His presence on the covenant people. Verse 33 reads, "Therefore having been exalted to the right hand of God, and having received from the Father the promise of the Holy Spirit, He [Christ] has poured forth this which you both see and hear."

The Holy Spirit is given in lavish measure. He is a pledge of things to come. He is our encourager and comforter. He dwells in the hearts of all God's people.

Verse 36 tells us one last thing about the Lord and host of the feast. He is the Christ—the Messiah. *Messiah* means "anointed one." Jesus was anointed with God's Holy Spirit. And when He passed on His Spirit to us, we became "anointed ones" as well. That is what the word *Christian* literally means.

I have a daughter-in-law named Christina, which means "little Christ." And in a real sense, each Christian is a "little Christ," a little "anointed one." I also have a grandson named Christopher. Christopher means "Christ-bearer" or "Christ carrier." Each Christian becomes a bearer of the Christ—a bearer of His anointing. We become Christinas and Christophers.

How generous and kind we find the Host of the feast. It is He who sits at the head of the table, at the right hand of God, and intercedes for us, His guests.

The Guests at the Feast

Notice the invitation extended in verses 37-47. Who received an invitation to the feast? It is no fun being left out. But this invitation carries good news. It has gone out through all the earth. Men everywhere are invited to this feast. Jesus Himself, the Lord of the feast, extends the invitation in Matthew 11:28-30: "Come to Me, all who are weary and heavy-laden, and I will give you rest. Take My yoke upon you, and learn from Me, for I am gentle and humble in heart; and you shall find rest for your souls. For My yoke is easy, and My load is light."

People from all over the ancient world gathered at Pentecost and heard Peter preach. Verse 37 tells of the response. After listening to Peter's invitation, they were "pierced to the heart."

They said to the apostles, "What shall we do?"

They had been *invited to the new harvest.* But the invitation did not stop with them. Verse 39 tells us, "For the promise is for you and your children, and for all who are far off." The harvest is for people of every culture and generation. All are *invited to enjoy a new deliverance.* The old deliverance centered in the law; the new deliverance centers in the cross. The old gave release from an external enemy—Egypt; the new gives freedom from the internal enemy—sin. This new deliverance is a once-for-all deliverance. It frees us from sin and death and releases us to eternal life in Jesus Christ.

Finally, Peter invited his audience to receive the new deliverance.How? Look at verse 38. Peter said to them in response to their question, "Repent, and let each of you be baptized in the name of Jesus Christ for the forgiveness of your sins; and you shall receive the gift of the Holy Spirit." Then in one final plea, he called, "Be saved from this perverse generation!" (v. 40).

That invitation is for all people. How will you respond? Receiving the invitation and acting on it means sharing in a feast of life. It begins with repentance; and once inside the banquet hall of God's presence, men sup with the Lord Himself.

The last part of chapter 2 speaks of the activities of the feast: the guests devoted themselves to the apostles' teaching, fellowship, and prayer, and shared their possessions (v. 42). It was a new life of loving God and enjoying Him forever (v. 46).

Jesus promised the Samaritan woman living water—water that would satisfy her thirst, water that springs up to eternal life. He told the multitude He was the Bread of Life. How will you respond to the Lord of the feast? What will you do with His invitation to drink and eat the feast of salvation?

Pentecost is not over. The Holy Spirit has not departed. The feast has never ended. The call still goes out to men and women everywhere to repent and believe on the Lord Jesus Christ.

Respond to His invitation now. Take time and consider what you will say to the Lord of the feast.

Remember

Pentecost was one of the feasts of Israel celebrating the blessing of God's presence.

The occasion of the Pentecost feast was a birthday—the birthday of the church.

In Acts 2, each man hears the gospel in his own language. Pentecost reversed the conditions resulting from the Tower of Babel.

The same power that delivered Jesus from the grave is available to the people of God today.

The invitation to the feast must go out to all the earth. Men everywhere are invited.

Questions

1. Give the Jewish meanings of Pentecost and compare them with the Christian meaning.
2. What is meant by the idea that Pentecost reversed the conditions left by the Tower of Babel?
3. How was Pentecost actually a birthday party?
4. What qualifies Jesus to be the Host (or Lord) of the feast?
5. What makes the invitation to this feast special?

Assignment

Looking at Leviticus 23 and Deuteronomy 16 and using a Bible dictionary, discover how the Old Testament Jews celebrated the feast of Pentecost. Draw parallels between that feast and the New Testament feast.

Acts 3
What Would You Say to a Beggar?

It is our care for the helpless, our practice of loving kindness, that brands us in the eyes of many of our opponents. "Look!" they say. "How they love one another! Look how they are prepared to die for one another."

— Tertullian

A recent study published in *Psychology Today* estimated that more than 2 million people live on our nation's streets. "Street people" include runaway children, immigrants, bag ladies, displaced families, alcoholics, drug addicts, the unemployed, the diseased, and the mentally ill. They are homeless people, reduced to begging, stealing, and scavenger hunting.

It happens in our cities a thousand times every day. You are in a hurry for an appointment, and you are already late. Suddenly, right in your path appears a beggar—hungry and homeless.

Or perhaps you are removed from the city. Someone calls in the middle of a busy day. It might be a friend, an acquaintance, or even your child. They need help, and they need it now. But you have things to do. Deadlines! A boss breathing down your neck, a golden opportunity, a fantastic sale, maybe even work for your church or another Christian cause. What do you do? How do you respond?

A similar encounter took place in Acts 3. Right in the middle of the church's rapid growth, Peter and John had their ministry interrupted by a beggar near the Temple in Jerusalem. Peter and John were forced to stop their hectic pace and to consider the needs of a disabled man. They stopped, looked, and then began to serve. Observe for a moment how Peter and John responded to that pressing need.

We discover four central figures in Acts 3: a beggar, two disciples, and the person and power of Jesus Christ. The beggar was suffering from a serious birth defect. The disciples stopped to help him. They served him, and their service pointed to Jesus Christ, the Suffering Servant.

Chapter 3 gives us a beautiful picture of the Christian servant.

THE SUFFERING MAN

The crowds of Acts 2 have dispersed. The great texts on church growth and world evangelism almost seem interrupted. Instead, our attention is directed to a lame man. He was born with a serious birth defect, which no doubt caused great discomfort and inconvenience. His condition made employment impossible, so begging seemed to be his only choice.

Someone set him down at the Temple gate. He arrived at three o'clock in the afternoon, the hour of prayer in the Temple. There would be many people there. Along with the other beggars, he probably thought, "If anyone will care for us, the people who claim to serve God will!"

Who can fault his thinking? He was absolutely right! If anyone ought to care, it is the people of God.

The disciples of Jesus had not yet pulled away from the national Temple worship. In Acts 3 we see Peter and John carrying out their duties as messianic Jews. It is a classic situation. Peter and John were going to pray. They were involved in the mechanics of their faith. What more pressing duty is there than the worship of God in prayer?

Then, just as they were about to enter the Temple, they came face-to-face with a suffering man. What would you do in a situation like that? Would you look the other way? Would you pass him by? Undoubtedly Jesus' parable of the Good Samaritan was fresh in their minds.

Verse 4 reads, "Peter, along with John, fixed his gaze upon

him and said, 'Look at us!' "

Consider how you might respond to the beggars on your path. You may say, "This hardly applies to me. Our community has no street people." But there are other kinds of beggars. Some want money, but others want life. Some beg for food and others for love and attention. Still others are looking for a listening ear. Can we, like Peter, fix our eyes on them?

One of my sons recently told me of two students at seminary. One was studious; the other was so distressed that he could barely study. He appeared to have no real friends, and his marriage was strained. In a shocking string of events, his mind snapped, and he killed his wife. But a few weeks before the tragic event, he was drawn to the other student because of a kind gesture toward him. In fact, he clung to him awkwardly.

And yet, rather than stopping to listen, the studious seminarian ignored him. He did not take time to listen.

He shut him out.

Shortly after the school term ended, the withdrawn student exploded in rage and violence.

Have you heard the cries of those around you? The beggars of life are not just on the streets of our cities but everywhere in our neighborhoods.

Perhaps you identify not with the disciples but with the suffering lame man. Like Peter, I would point you to Christ Jesus, the Suffering Servant, who is sufficient for every need. It was the name of Jesus (v. 16) that strengthened this man and brought him wholeness. It is in Jesus' name alone that there is power and forgiveness.

Peter proclaims in verse 19, "Repent therefore and return, that your sins may be wiped away, in order that times of refreshing may come from the presence of the Lord."

SERVANT-DISCIPLES

Turning our attention from the suffering man, we come next to the two servant-disciples, Peter and John. The text does not explicitly call these disciples "servants." But that is exactly what they were. A servant is one who gives himself to another in need.

What were the needs at hand? They were physical—the man was crippled. They were also spiritual—the man lacked the wholeness that only Jesus gives. Some might want to lay emphasis on one or the other, but the Holy Spirit tells us of both.

The thrust of Acts is its focus on sharing the good news; evangelism is on every page. Chapter 3 is no different. The disciples wanted to share the most valuable possession they had, and that was Jesus Christ.

Nevertheless, we cannot isolate gospel preaching from gospel living. When we do that we hinder the gospel. Preaching and living go together. That is why the episode with the beggar comes on the heels of the great story of Pentecost.

The question of Acts is not a question of evangelism versus social responsibility. The two are intimately bound. The question is rather: Are disciples of Jesus consistent in word and *deed?* Peter and John practiced an evangelism of love. They did not disown the suffering man. Rather, they acted in a way that affirmed their prayers for the lost.

What about you? Do you disown the suffering ones? Does need repel or attract you? What does your church do when it learns of a crisis in the neighborhood? Does your business or local government ignore the neediest members of your community?

It is one thing for Christians to argue against a welfare state. But if it does nothing to help those in earnest need who otherwise depend on government, then its politics are cruel. In a time of government cutbacks in social programs the church has a golden opportunity to volunteer for the service of the *whole* man. The time is right for the church to touch the needy with the hands of Jesus.

During World War II, a church in Strasbourg, France, was destroyed. Little remained but rubble. When the rubble was cleared, a statue of Christ, standing erect, was found. It was unbroken except for the two hands, which were missing. In time, the church was rebuilt.

A sculptor, noticing the missing hands on the statue of Christ, said, "Let me carve a new statue of Christ, with hands."

Church officials met to consider the sculptor's proposal. His offer was rejected. A spokesman for the church said, "Our broken statue will serve to remind us that Christ touches the hearts of men, but He has no hands to minister to the needy or feed the hungry or enrich the poor *except our hands.*"

Peter and John did not disown the suffering man. They acted as servants for Christ's sake. The Holy Spirit brought a change in their behavior.

What else did the disciples offer the beggar? The lame man was expecting money. But in verse 6 Peter says, "I do not possess silver and gold, but what I do have I give to you: in the name of Jesus Christ the Nazarene—walk!" Peter had been given a gift of preaching and healing. Healing was a unique apostolic gift. Peter gave of the gifts that he had.

Can you also say, "What I do have I give to you"? Just as there are all kinds of beggars, so there are all kinds of givers. God has uniquely endowed each of His children with gifts and talents. What has He given you? Faith? Money? A gift of hospitality? A strong body? The ability to encourage? Teaching gifts?

I do not know your gift, but I do know that you are gifted. I do not know your particular call to service, but I do know that as a Christian you are called to be a servant. Remember this: when the church stops giving, it loses its power. When the church stops serving, it almost always starts swerving—into the wrong lane.

The early church was a servant church, and the evidence of its service was its power. Peter and John realized that service was not an elective but rather a required course for every Christian. It is not an endowment of the clergy but rather the rent every Christian should pay for the space we occupy on God's earth. Peter and John were servants, and we are too. What are you giving in the name of Christ?

SUFFERING AND SERVICE IN BALANCE

Jesus was the chief of servants. Ask anyone to list the greatest people who ever lived. The list usually begins with Jesus because He gave Himself for others. In Acts 3, Luke first applies the title *servant* to Jesus: "God raised up His servant, and sent Him to bless you" (v. 26). Jesus was God's Servant Messiah, sent with a mission.

But that is not what the priests of Jerusalem were expecting. They waited for a Messiah who would reign in kingly splendor. Even the disciples expected Christ to come in political triumph freeing the Jews from Roman rule. Jesus turned all those expectations on their heads. Jesus said, "Whoever wishes to become great among you shall be your *servant*" (Matthew 20:26, emphasis added).

But not only was Jesus the Chief Servant—He was also a Suffering Servant. When Luke called Jesus God's Servant, he drew from the prophecy of Isaiah. Isaiah vividly described the servant of Jehovah: "He was despised and forsaken of men, a man of sorrows, and acquainted with grief; and like one from whom men hide their face, He was despised and we did not esteem Him" (Isaiah 53:3).

The apostles took that to be a prophecy about Jesus. On the cross, He was rejected by men and forsaken by the Father. He felt the loneliness of desertion and the agony of crucifixion.

What did Jesus offer to His disciples? It was not a place of honor. It was a rugged cross. Our Lord's triumph came in dying. The cross preceded the crown. His call to us is to come and die—to our sins and the stubbornness of our rebellious hearts.

It is popular today to preach a gospel of self-affirmation and self-esteem. Go into any bookstore, and you will find shelves filled with positive self-image books. But Jesus pointed to a way of self-denial. It is by dying to yourself that you find yourself.

Remember the life of the apostle Paul? Here was a man educated to become a religious leader. A bright, comfortable future lay before him. Yet when he met Jesus, he discovered something was missing in that way of life. He gave up the comfort and convenience of being a scholar. He chose to bypass the companionship of a wife. Instead he became a persecuted, hunted, traveling preacher. However, in forsaking himself and doing what Christ wanted, he found fulfillment and satisfaction in life.

If this were the end of our story, it would be a sad ending. Jesus would then be no different from any other sufferer. But the message of verse 16 is that the name of Jesus brings forgiveness to those who suffer. That is what makes Jesus' service and suffering so unique. It brought life from death and turned mourning into rejoicing. He took our sins upon Himself and gave us His righteousness.

Isaiah wrote of the Suffering Servant, "Surely our griefs He Himself bore, and our sorrows He carried . . . He was pierced through for our transgressions, He was crushed for our iniquities; the chastening for our well-being fell upon Him, and by His scourging we are healed" (Isaiah 53:4-5).

What makes the empty cross a symbol of hope? Simply this: the suffering service of a sinless Man overcame our sin and death. Death was momentary. It gave way to a resurrection of life.

That is the hope that Peter and John offered the lame man. The name of our risen Lord enables beggars of all walks of life to rise up, to leap, and to praise the living God.

Remember

The needy are all around us: many people need attention, love, and someone to listen to them.

God has no hands to meet those needs but ours.

Jesus calls us to a life of self-denial—the only way to find ourselves.

Questions

1. Identify those around you in need, begging for your help.
2. What is your special area of service? Are you making the best use of that ability?
3. Are your acts of kindness pointing others to Christ or to yourself?
4. Identify areas of your life that need to be given over to Christ.

Assignment

Identify ways you can make use of your gifts and abilities to serve someone that you know desperately needs help. How can you be more sensitive to the needs of those around you in order that you may serve them better?

Acts 4
The Power of a Holy Life

There is no sight so sublime, no power so resistless, as that man or woman who lives a holy life.
— George Sweeting

Holiness is not mystical speculation, and it is not found in monastic retreat. It is neither enthusiastic fervor nor scrupulous keeping of the law. None of those separately or corporately define holiness.

Holiness is first and foremost a quality of life that comes from trusting and obeying Jesus Christ. It is the result of God's character rubbing off on our character. It comes when Jesus and the Holy Spirit are the primary molding influences on our lives.

Holiness cannot be, as Charles Colson puts it, "the private preserve of an elite corps of martyrs, mystics and Nobel Prize winners." To the contrary, holiness is the everyday business of everyday Christians. Holy living is the net result of communion with our Lord.

There is no power in this world quite like the power of a holy life. Leonard Ravenhill put it in this way: "The greatest miracle that God can do today is to take an unholy man out of an unholy world, and make him holy . . . and then put him back into that unholy world, and keep him there." That is the miracle that marked the lives of the disciples of Jesus in Acts 4.

Here we see two disciples, Peter and John, dragged before the great Temple court in Jerusalem. In the name of Jesus, they had just healed a lame beggar at the Temple gate. You can imagine the stir it caused. When Peter told the people that the resurrection power of Jesus healed the man, a riot nearly occurred. By referring to Jesus, the disciples touched a tender nerve in the Sadducees and the priests. The Sadducees rejected any possibility of resurrection. The priests, Annas and Caiaphas, only a few weeks earlier had taken part in the condemnation of Jesus. Talk of resurrection or healing in Jesus' name was the last thing they wanted to hear. However, the proof of the miracle was overwhelming. A man who had been lame for more than forty years was now walking.

Perhaps you can feel the tenseness of the situation. Peter and John, commoners, standing before the highest court in the land, faced the toughest lawyers and most brilliant theologians of that day. Worse yet, the leaders were furious over the trouble these two were making in their city.

What caused Peter and John to stand out on this occasion? How is it that those two ordinary men displayed greater influence than the best and the brightest of their generation? The answer is that they were holy men of God. Their lives were dramatically transformed by the resurrection of Jesus. They were trusting in the Son of God, obeying His commands, and as a result, they experienced Holy Spirit power.

THE FOUNDATION OF HOLINESS

Let's consider the foundation of their holiness. We read about it in verses 1-12. The rulers question Peter and John asking, "By what power, or in what name, have you done this?" (v. 7).

Their answer was direct: "Rulers and elders of the people . . . let it be known to all of you, and to all the people of Israel, that by the name of Jesus Christ the Nazarene, whom you crucified, whom God raised from the dead—by this name this man stands here before you in good health" (vv. 8-10).

Peter said that the name and the power of the miracle belong together. They belong to Jesus.

The name of Jesus stood for an authoritative power. Names always stand for something. We see the connection between one's name and one's power for authority in government.

Prior to the 1984 election, presidential candidate Walter Mondale met with Soviet foreign minister Andrei Gromyko. It was an awkward meeting. Mondale was only a candidate and had to speak supportively of President Reagan's policies. Mondale said to the Soviet leader, "President Reagan is our president and there should be no misunderstanding about that." By involving the president's name, Mondale reminded Gromyko that Reagan's name stood for the recent increase in American military power. Gromyko understood that well. The Soviets knew that the name *Reagan* stood behind American foreign policy, and they knew it represented a formidable power.

That is precisely the point that Peter made. The name of Jesus stood for a formidable power. Without that name, there is no power.

First, Jesus' name speaks of the power of salvation. In verse 12, Peter upsets the Temple court. He warned them that apart from Jesus, "there is no other name under heaven . . . by which we must be saved." All the religion in the world cannot save a man from his sins. Yet that is what the rulers believed. They said, "Keep the law and you will be holy." For them, holiness began with human works, and salvation was attained by effort. That seems to be the philosophy of today: do the best you can, try not to harm your fellow man, and everything will come out OK.

But Peter and John claimed that that path is a dead end. The way of good works is not the way to holiness. Rather, holiness is the way to good works. Holiness is first a gift given by God through Christ. It comes from trusting Jesus' saving righteousness. For Peter, holiness began when he met and trusted Jesus. Thereafter, it grew by obeying Him.

Second, the name of Jesus referred to the power of Christian living. Peter's holiness was not the result of a one-time injection. It came, rather, from a daily dose. Unlike a jump-start for a battery that needs only an occasional charge, it was a steady current that came from being wired into the Light of the world.

Popular today are hand-held, portable vacuum cleaners. Those handy little devices can easily be carried through the house for light cleaning. However, they must always return to the holder designed for them in order to receive another charge. Their power is not like that of the normal vacuum cleaner, which, when connected to an outlet, has continuous power.

Continual fellowship with Christ provides the constant power we need for living. As we walk with Him and obey Him, our lives will begin to shine. Holiness becomes a "throbbing, pulsating connection with the divine dynamo" (W. T. Purkiser).

Twice in chapter 4 we are told that Peter and John followed God's holy Servant. The source of their holiness was Jesus, and everything they did was done in His name. In verse 10 it says they healed the lame man in Jesus' name; in verse 18 they teach in Jesus' name; in verse 30 they work in Jesus' name.

Whose name and power will you draw upon this week? It seems that there are two ruts we must avoid. The first might be called "blind Christianity," and the second we will call "dumb Christianity."

Blind Christianity characterizes those who claim to be Jesus' disciples but have no deeds to prove it. No one can see their faith lived out. People are blind to its reality. Christianity is all talk and no action.

Dumb Christianity, on the other hand, comes from those who are rich in good deeds but never act in a definite name. For all others know, you might be a secular humanist or a hard-working Mormon. But who will ever know the source of your love if you do not speak the name?

Peter and John avoided both tendencies. Their witness was clear. They served others in the unmistakable name of Jesus. That was the foundation of their holiness.

THE MARKS OF HOLINESS

With that foundation in mind, let us look at some marks of holiness. Verses 13-37 suggest six marks of a holy life. These marks show that the holy life involves more than just living a religious life-style.

The first mark is that *it cannot be explained*. Jesus told Nicodemus that the Holy Spirit is like the wind: He defies human explanation. So it is with a holy life. Verse 13 states that Peter and John, "uneducated and untrained men," shocked the religious doctors of their day. They spoke with deep insight about the things of God.

Recall the story of Jesus in the Temple as recorded in John 7:15. The Jews asked, "How has this man become learned, having never been educated?" Jesus responded, "My teaching is not mine, but His Who sent me" (v. 16). So it was with Peter and John.

Jesus' ministry could not be explained and neither could the disciples'. The same has been true with all holy people down through the ages. Martin Luther was a despairing monk, William Carey a cobbler, D. L. Moody a shoe salesman. Yet Luther became a great church reformer, Carey a mighty missionary, and Moody an evangelist. Those and thousands of others have been transformed and taught by the Holy Spirit of God. The lives of Peter and John defied all human explanation. That is a mark of a holy life.

A second mark is that *it cannot be argued with*. Verses 14-16 convey the dilemma of the opposition: "What shall we do with these men? For the fact that a noteworthy miracle has taken place through them is apparent to all who live in Jerusalem, and we cannot deny it."

Take, for example, the conversion of Charles Colson, former special counsel to President Nixon, convicted and sent to prison for his Watergate activities in the mid-1970s. The press handled his conversion story with suspicion. People were skeptical about whether his conversion was genuine or not. Many thought that his work with prisoners after being released from jail was a tactic to win sympathy. By the 1980s the critics changed their tune. Cynicism was gone. A major news magazine simply called him "the founder of Prison Fellowship and a lay Christian minister." His life speaks for itself. It cannot be argued with.

In the case of the lame man, the Temple leaders could not afford to be skeptics. The man was now walking and leaping. You see, a man with an argument is always at the mercy of a man with a genuine experience. A holy life, be it the life of the lame man, Peter, or any true believer, cannot be argued with. It is simply there as its own witness, and people have to deal with it.

That leads us to the third mark of a holy life: its obedience is so persistent that *it cannot be intimidated.* It revolutionizes its environment. Lock it away, and it transforms the prison; kill it, and its blood will become the seed of the church.

Joe Butts went out as a pioneer missionary to the mountain village of El Carman, Colombia. He founded an elementary school and began a Bible study. Hostility in the village grew and he was forced to leave the area. Ten years later Joe returned to El Carman, where there had been no missionary for over a decade. There he found several churches with fifty to one hundred members each, and many smaller congregations in the surrounding countryside. Though persecution existed, the holy life of the believers could not be constrained.

Look at Peter. He faced two threats. The first was fear. The last time Peter was near the Jewish court he had been cursing and denying his relationship with Jesus. The change was dramatic. Now Peter would not miss an opportunity to speak in Jesus' name.

The second threat was the government. They commanded Peter and John not to teach in Jesus' name. The answer of the two disciples is in verse 19: "Whether it is right in the sight of God to give heed to you rather than to God, you be the judge; for we cannot stop speaking what we have seen and heard." That is a mark of holiness. It cannot stop speaking about Jesus. It cannot be contained.

A fourth mark of a holy life is that *it cannot be at home in this city.* Look at verse 27. The verse speaks about the city's opposition to Jesus. Luke writes, "For truly in this city there were gathered together against Thy holy servant Jesus . . . both Herod and Pontius Pilate, along with the Gentiles and the peoples of Israel." In verse 29 Peter prays, "And now, Lord, take note of their threats." Peter's holiness caused the same disturbance as did Jesus' holiness. People opposed all that they stood for.

Holy men are called to be in the world but not of the world. They reside in the city of man, but they are ultimately committed to the city of God. Do you see the tension?

Sometimes Christians lose their holiness when they become too much at home in the city of man. Between A.D. 312 and 410, the Christian church won a major victory. The faith was embraced by the Roman emperor Constantine. By 395, Christianity was officially recognized as the religion of the Roman Empire. What a triumph it seemed! With the church practically ruling the city of Rome, nothing seemed beyond its grasp. Then in 410, in a jolt that shook the ancient world, at the height of the church's political success, Rome was sacked by the Visigoths. In response to that great defeat Augustine wrote *The City of God*. There he reminds the church that God's city is an eternal one that can never be too closely tied with the city of man.

Of course, there is an opposite danger too. Some Christians run to monasteries to escape the world. At times they are real monasteries. But often they are cloisters of church activity. They build their own Christian ghettos and withdraw from their commission to go into all the world and make disciples.

But look at the holiness of Peter. It was not at home in this city. But it remained in the city, because that is what Jesus commanded. Peter's separation from the world was spiritual and not physical. If it was physical there would be no one left to minister to the cities in Jesus' name. Peter's holiness drove him into the city for Christ's sake. His holiness disturbed the city. How about yours?

The fifth mark of holiness is that *it cannot stop praying.* Verses 24-31 tell of Peter and John in prayer with the other disciples. What do they pray for? They pray for boldness in their witness, that God will work through them. Verse 31 reads, "And when they had prayed, the place where they had gathered together was shaken, and they were all filled with the Holy Spirit, and began to speak the word of God with boldness."

Not long ago I visited some of the churches in Korea. I had heard many different reports as to what I might find. But what I found was a praying church. Korean Christians have been called the Olympic champions of the world in prayer. On every morning of the week Christians can be seen in the early mist of daybreak walking to church with their songbooks and Bibles. Early morning prayer meeting begins at 4:30 A.M. in churches across the nation.

Those meetings generate the electricity that has lighted the Korean church today.

Warren Wiersbe says that one of the most moving experiences of his life came when he stepped from John Wesley's bedroom in his London home into the little adjacent prayer room. Outside the house was the traffic of the city road, but inside was the hush of God. Its only furnishings were a walnut table that held a Greek New Testament, a candlestick, a small stool, and a chair. When he was in London, Wesley entered that room early each morning to read God's Word and pray. The guide said to Dr. Wiersbe, "This little room was the powerhouse of Methodism."

What is the powerhouse in your home and life? Where is such commitment in this so-called "age of the evangelical"? The mark of a holy life is that it cannot stop praying.

A sixth and final mark is found in the fact that a holy life *cannot stop giving.* Verse 32 states that the congregation was of one heart and soul, "and not one of them claimed that anything belonging to him was his own; but all things were common property to them."

These verses have been misinterpreted by many. Some see here a form of Christian Communism. But a casual reading of the New Testament will not support that—certain disciples had homes and possessions. Others see these verses as supporting a Christian right to private property. But that too misses the point. What is described in these verses is the Christian's right to private stewardship. We own nothing. It is on loan to us. It is loaned for a purpose: to serve others in Jesus' name. That is what the early church was doing.

Verse 34 says that there was not a needy person among them. That is because the church had such a sense of stewardship that its members would not let anyone go in need.

Karl Marx was borrowing from Christian principles when he decreed, "From each according to his abilities, to each according to his needs." That principle is here in our text.

In 1892 Fredrich Engels, a socialist collaborator with Marx, wrote his book *Socialism: Utopian and Scientific.* In the introduction, Engels criticized religion because it did nothing to help the plight of the needy. Engels even referred to the revivalism of Moody and the Salvation Army as examples of religious ineffectiveness in dealing with social questions. It has almost been one hundred years since Engels wrote that. Since then, many of our social scientists have concluded that the great socialistic experiment has run its course. Nevertheless, the *problems* to which Engels and Marx and Moody were addressing still remain. What an opportunity the church has to offer our world a love that cannot stop giving.

John Wesley passionately argued that there could be "no holiness but social holiness . . . [and] to turn Christianity into a solitary religion is to destroy it."

But look at the example of the church in Acts 4. They were stewards in Christ's name. They could not stop giving. They overflowed with love. As a result, verse 33 reads, "with great power the apostles were giving witness to the resurrection of the Lord Jesus, and abundant grace was upon them all." Their giving and their love commanded their witness to Christ.

What kind of a giver are you? The disciples were marked by a holy love that could not stop giving. They were cheerful givers. The mark of a holy life is that it cannot stop giving.

All of these were marks of active holiness in the early Christian church. It was a vibrant, relevant holiness that came from believing on the Lord Jesus Christ. That is the enlightening, active holiness that our world must see again.

There is no power in the world quite like the power of a holy life. May God enable us to pursue such a life.

Remember

"The greatest miracle that God can do today is to take an unholy man out of an unholy world and make him holy . . . and then put him back into that unholy world, and keep him there" (Leonard Ravenhill).

Holiness is first and foremost a quality of life that comes from trusting and obeying Jesus Christ.

Power for Christian living is not the result of a one-time injection but a daily dose.

Questions

1. Why would talk of the resurrection cause a near riot in Jerusalem?
2. In what ways did Peter and John use the name of Jesus?
3. Peter and John prayed for boldness and that God would work through them. How can I make those prayers a part of my prayer life? How can I act on those prayers?
4. In what ways has my giving been a demonstration of my Christian life this past week?

Assignment

Discover ways you could have or should have drawn on the power of Jesus' name during the past week. Commit your life fully to God and claim the power of Jesus' name in leading a holy life each day.

Acts 5
The Ghost of Achan

I shall tell you a great secret, my friend. Do not wait for the
last judgment, it takes place every day.
— Albert Camus

Can a Christian get away with sin? Some people seem to think
so. However, a closer look points to another answer. God is
always opposed to sin. He is never deceived and cannot be out-
witted. He may allow sin to continue for a time, but there will be
a day of accountability.

Nothing leads to evil quite as much as the idea that this
world is all there is. Those who commit violent crimes and who
harm the innocent have usually first convinced themselves that
there will never be a day of judgment. Even the motorist speeding down the highway has convinced himself he will not receive
a speeding ticket.

However, Jesus says that people who believe they will never be found out are wrong: "There is nothing covered up that
will not be revealed, and hidden that will not be known" (Luke
12:2).

A Sunday school teacher once was telling the story from
Luke 16 about the rich man and Lazarus. She told how Lazarus
the beggar had little in life but was rich in faith. Ultimately he
died and was taken to the bosom of Abraham. The rich man had
everything in this life but faith. Ultimately, he died and was sepa-
rated from God.

Then the Sunday school teacher turned to her pupils and

asked, "Now which would you choose?" One child spoke up and answered, "I want to be the rich man while he lived and Lazarus when he died."

But we cannot have it both ways. At death the rich man discovered the truth of Numbers 32:23: "Be sure your sin will find you out." That phrase is not an idle statement, a witty proverb, or a piece of fatherly advice. Rather, it is a law of God, a principle of Scripture voiced repeatedly in the Bible.

For example, Hosea 8:7 reads, "For they sow the wind, and they reap the whirlwind." Jesus declares in His Sermon on the Mount in Matthew 7:2, "And by your standard of measure, it will be measured to you." Paul writes in Galatians 6:7, "Do not be deceived, God is not mocked; for whatever a man sows, this he will also reap."

The Old Testament book of Joshua, chapter 7, describes the sin of a man named Achan. In an act of disobedience, he stole and lied. As a result of his sin, Israel suffered a humiliating defeat in battle for the city of Ai.

A similar situation arose in Acts 5 that hindered the early church. Two members, Ananias and Sapphira, lied to Peter and to the Holy Spirit. In both our Old and New Testament examples God delivered the swift retribution of sudden death.

In Acts, the infant apostolic church was forcefully reminded that the law of reaping applies not only to unbelievers but also to believers: in this case, Ananias and Sapphira. Chapter 5 records their sudden death. It reminds us that internal church problems are often more serious than external ones. The church expected and prepared for danger from without. Acts 4 speaks of the external threat of persecution and how the church responded to it. Persecution drove them to their knees. The courage of believers increased, and the number of followers multiplied. Instead of destroying the church, its enemies helped build it by bitter persecution.

Having failed at external opposition, Satan next attacked internally. Acts 4 closes with an account of Barnabas, a man who had just closed a real estate transaction. He had a family estate on the island of Cyprus that he put up for sale. Instead of putting the proceeds in the First National Bank of Jerusalem, he brought the money to the apostles for the needs of the church.

Such generous giving was characteristic of the early church: "For there was not a needy person among them, for all who were owners of land or houses would sell them and bring the proceeds of the sales, and lay them at the apostles' feet" (Acts 4:34). All who were owners wanted to share and did so of their own free will. No one told Barnabas to sell his land and give the proceeds to the church. It was not a rule of the church. The Holy Spirit, who is the Spirit of unselfishness, was working so that those who had possessions considered nothing as their own.

This same principle holds true today. All that I have belongs to God. Occasionally we sing:

> Naught that I have I call my own,
> I hold it for the giver.
> My life, my soul, my will, my *all*
> Are His, and His forever.

The giving of the early church was not by regulation but was rather the natural, spontaneous outcome of the Spirit-filled life.

Even in that setting of mutual giving the great generosity of Barnabas brought immediate recognition. Undoubtedly the entire church was talking about his kindness (Acts 4:36-37).

Acts 5, however, begins with the word *but,* which suggests a contrast: "But a certain man named Ananias, with his wife Sapphira, sold a piece of property and kept back some of the price."

THE SIN THAT THREATENED THE CHURCH

Ananias and Sapphira probably witnessed the recognition given Barnabas and others. They also owned some property, and they probably desired a share of the praise. What was their sin? They wanted credit for giving all when they only gave a part. Their sin was that they portrayed a greater dedication than they really had.

There is no question that Ananias and Sapphira had talked the situation over. They were not willing to give all their assets. To give everything would be going a little too far. Maybe they thought of their children's education, which would make demands on the family bank account. Possibly they were concerned about their own future, looking forward to retirement.

Consider the setting. The Jerusalem church was in the midst of a crisis. The judgment of God was hanging over the city, and Jerusalem was about to be destroyed. As Jesus predicted, not one stone would be left upon another. The church was short on funds. Argument over the Gentile question began to cause division. In such a time, some of the Jerusalem Christians were saying, "We'll sell what we have to aid world evangelization."

Barnabas probably led the way, and the people became excited at the prospect of sharing the gospel. Ananias and Sapphira probably thought, "We'd better get in on this, but let's not go all the way. Let's pretend to give all."

They could have come to the leaders of the church and explained just how they felt. "We'd like to give some, but we need to keep some for a rainy day." In all probability, that would have been acceptable. Instead, they schemed to get credit for giving all when they had given only a part. They were under no obligation to sell, nor were they under any obligation to give. Their deep, dark sin was lying and hypocrisy. As a result, their sin threatened the oneness and power of the early church.

The apostle Peter did not waste words. "Ananias, why has Satan filled your heart to lie to the Holy Spirit?" (v. 3). It is a dangerous thing to lie to God.

Proverbs 6:17-19 provides a list of seven things that God hates, two of which involve outright deceit, the others a deceitful heart: "Haughty eyes, a lying tongue, and hands that shed innocent blood, a heart that devises wicked plans, feet that run rapidly to evil, a false witness who utters lies, and one who spreads strife among brothers."

The Bible teaches that God hates lying, fraud, embezzlement, slander, libel, and breach of promise—all products of a lying heart. From where does lying come? Jesus gave the answer when He said to the religious leaders, "You are of your father the devil" (John 8:44).

About three hours after the death of Ananias, Sapphira came along. The text gives no indication why she had not been with her husband when he was confronted by Peter. Possibly she wanted praise for herself. In any case, she entered, expecting honor, praise, and recognition.

Peter immediately asked her, "Tell me whether you sold the land for such and such a price?" And she said, "Yes, that was the price" (v. 8).

Peter's response was blunt. "Why is it that you have agreed together to put the Spirit of the Lord to the test? Behold, the feet of those who have buried your husband are at the door, and they shall carry you out as well" (v. 9).

Marriage is a beautiful union. But it is sad when a husband and wife join together to lie to God. Sapphira should have said, "Ananias, this is wrong! We can't deceive God or the church. I love you but I can't cooperate." Thank God for the husband or wife who will not take the path of least resistance but rather stand for that which they know is right.

Verse 10 tells us that Sapphira, like her husband, died at Peter's feet. She was carried out and buried next to Ananias. Verse 11 adds, "And great fear came upon the whole church." The church needs some of that same fear today. Too many church members are careless with the truth and deceive freely. They lack a fear of God.

THE SEVERITY THAT SAVED THE CHURCH

The swift stroke of judgment in Acts 5 was meant to reveal God's holiness and opposition to deceit and sin. The penalty was severe, and it was so for a reason. Ananias and Sapphira disrupted the blessing and power of the early church. They brought into the church the same corruption that Adam and Eve brought into the human race.

The severity of Acts 5 was a one-time situation. God did not continue to impose immediate death for every lie and act of deception. If He had, an abnormal situation would have resulted. The moral sense of Christians would have disappeared and obedience would have been given purely out of fear.

The punishment of sudden death for Ananias and Sapphira, in spite of its severity, was essentially an act of mercy. It saved the early church from carelessness and corruption. Defilement of the church by sin would have been far more tragic than the deaths of the two involved.

Acts 5 stands as a pointed reminder that God totally opposes sin. Take a favorable attitude toward sin and God must take an unfavorable attitude toward you. No Christian can entertain sin and get away with it.

The Royal Canadian Mounted Police have taken as their motto, "We always get our man." The implication is that no matter where a wanted man runs, he will be found. Sin is the same way. No matter how hard we try, we cannot hide our sins. Regardless of how much good we do, it will not cover our disobedience.

God will not allow sin in the lives of His children to go unchecked. In 1 Corinthians 5:5 Paul writes of a certain Corinthian believer as being delivered unto Satan "for the destruction of his flesh, that his spirit may be saved in the day of the Lord Jesus."

He also tells us in 1 Corinthians 11 that weakness, sickness, and untimely deaths among that membership were because of careless abuses of the Table of the Lord. Verses 31-32 remind us, "If we judged ourselves rightly, we should not be judged. But when we are judged, we are disciplined by the Lord in order that we may not be condemned along with the world."

God wants us to be sensitive to personal purity and holiness. The writer of Hebrews reminds us that "The Lord will judge His people," and "it is a terrifying thing to fall into the hands of the living God" (Hebrews 10:30-31).

God expects congregations as well as individuals to deal with sin. In addressing the church at Ephesus in Revelation 2, Jesus warns, "Remember therefore from where you have fallen, and repent and do the deeds you did at first; or else I am coming to you, and will remove your lampstand out of its place—unless you repent" (v. 5).

Jesus gave the church at Ephesus two options—repent, or lose your light. Essentially He was saying that you cannot treat sin lightly and still expect God's blessing. Godly fear requires a life of humble obedience to Jesus Christ.

The ghost of Achan from the book of Joshua is seen in the lives of Ananias and Sapphira. The account of their story tells that the grace of God is no more tolerant of sin than the law of God. If you are living in sin, you are inviting God's chastening, and God deals with sin severely. Allow Jesus Christ to forgive you and to give you His power to live a godly life.

Remember

"There is nothing covered up that will not be revealed, and hidden that will not be known" (Luke 12:2). "Be sure your sin will find you out" (Numbers 32:23).

The giving of the early church was not by regulation but was rather the natural, spontaneous outcome of the Spirit-filled life.

The sin of Ananias and Sapphira was that they portrayed a greater dedication than they really had.

Take a favorable attitude toward sin and God must take an unfavorable attitude toward you.

Questions

1. Why can internal church problems be potentially more harmful than external persecution?
2. What caused the generosity of the believers in the closing verses of chapter 4?
3. What would have been the result if God had continued to impose immediate death for acts of deception? Why would that have been an unhealthy situation?

Assignment

List the similarities between Achan and Ananias and Sapphira. Analyze your own life and see where the similarities lie. Bring these to God in confession and covenant with Him to avoid them in the future.

Acts 6
Three Dangers
to a Growing Church

One hundred religious persons knit into a unity by careful organization do not constitute a church any more than eleven dead men make a football team. The first requisite is life, always.

— A. W. Tozer

The good news is that churches are growing. The bad news is that growth brings its own difficulties. That is the situation in the United States and in many countries of Asia and Africa. But it was also the case in Jerusalem shortly after Christ's death.

Churches come in all shapes and sizes.

There are small churches: a Baptist chapel in an English village, a house church in East Africa, or a storefront church in Los Angeles.

But there are also large churches. The Moody Memorial Church in Chicago seats more than 4,000 people. A church in Sao Paulo, Brazil, seats 25,000. In Korea, the Full Gospel Central Church has 270,000 members, and a Lutheran church in Africa has a membership of 500,000.

It is estimated that each day there are at least 78,000 men and women who become Christians on our planet. Right now, most of that growth is not in the West. Nevertheless, a recent Gallup report informs us that church attendance is up in North America as well.

That was also true in the Jerusalem church almost two thousand years ago. Here was the movement from which all contemporary church growth began. Acts 2 says that in one day during the Feast of Pentecost, more than three thousand believers were added to the church. In Acts 4, more than five thousand men believed. Acts 6:7 reads, "The number of the disciples continued to increase greatly in Jerusalem."

Imagine the excitement that growth generated. However, with the growth there were also dangers. In chapter 6, three such dangers stand out. The early church experienced the dangers of discrimination, professionalism, and neglect of the Word of God. These same dangers exist today.

THE DANGER OF DISCRIMINATION

First, let us consider the danger of discrimination. Acts 6:1 tells us that the number of disciples was increasing. Two groups of converts are mentioned: Greek Jews and native Hebrews. The Greek Jews were originally from outside of Palestine. After their conversion they were together with the native Christians in Jerusalem. A complaint arose between the two groups concerning fair treatment of the Greek widows.

Keep in mind the context. The gospel was about to cross the boundaries of Palestine. In chapters 6-9 we see the beginnings of a mission to the Greek-speaking world. Chapter 8 speaks of the spread of the church to Samaria and the conversion story of the Ethiopian. By chapter 9, Saul turns to Christ and starts down a path that makes him the great missionary to the Gentiles. Those chapters tell of missions. Evangelism was alive and well, and yet problems arose in that context.

Besides evangelism, verse 1 tells us of the church's responsibility to help the needy. In this case, it was the widows. The wealthier members of the congregation had contributed to a common fund. Each day the church would take something from that account and use it to help the widows. Both that earthly concern and the success of evangelism form a backdrop for understanding the first danger that confronted this growing church.

The problem began with the new kid in town. A different kind of person came to church. The congregation was no longer made exclusively of Palestinian Jews. There was an immigrant invasion from Greek-speaking lands. The Greek-speaking Jewish Christians did things differently. They spoke Greek and not the more common Palestinian language of Aramaic. That is the only difference our text mentions, but the language barrier illustrates the larger cultural barrier. Such barriers often lead to discrimination.

Many experienced ethnic discriminations when they first immigrated to the United States. Their accent differed from their neighbors; their native tongue was not English. They felt second class as a result. Sometimes those feelings were warranted and sometimes imagined. Either way, they felt discriminated against. The same was true in the early church—cultural barriers resulted in neglect and ultimately discord.

In the first half of this century, the question of racial discrimination in America's churches was a major threat to Christian unity. In 1974 presidential candidate Jimmy Carter told about the deacons of his church. They voted to eject any black person who sought to worship there. Carter went on to say how he opposed the move because it was contrary to the Scriptures.

There are other forms of discrimination as well. It may be that a poor church refuses wealthier Christians, or a cushy, elegant church has lost contact with the poor. It may be that the spiritual gifts of women are not recognized. It may be a thousand other things, but the point is, as Paul says, "there is no partiality with God" (Romans 2:11). No Jew or Greek; no slave or freeman; no male or female.

It need not be as blatant as language or race discrimination. Sometimes we discriminate merely because we resist change.

A certain small church was located in a rural community. As time passed the community began to attract a large number of retired couples. Some of them became active in the church. As time passed, certain of the long-time members hesitated to place the newcomers on the church board. "It's our church," they said, "and we don't want outsiders running it."

The mark of the Christian is love. The manifestation of our love to the world is Christian unity. When Christians start shunning or ignoring other Christians for unjust reasons, that unity is broken. Sadly, that fractures our witness to the world. As Christians we must avoid the dangers of discrimination.

THE DANGER OF PROFESSIONAL MINISTRY

There was a second danger facing the young, vibrant church in Jerusalem, the danger of professional ministry. We find it in 6:1-3.

The complaint about the widows being mistreated came before the apostles. Listen to their response: "It is not desirable for us to neglect the word of God in order to serve tables" (v. 2). The *New English Bible* reads, "It would be a grave mistake" for us to do this.

The offended ones went to the apostles, and rightly so. However, they went expecting the apostles to actually do the work themselves. Instead, the apostles threw the ball back to them saying, "Select from among you, brethren, seven men of good reputation, full of the Spirit and of wisdom, whom we may put in charge of this task" (v. 3). Ministry was not a job for the preachers only, but for all God's people.

Ephesians 4:11 teaches, "He gave some as . . . pastors and teachers, for the equipping of the saints for the work of service." What was the leader's role? To equip believers so that they could minister. In other words, a good pastor-teacher is like a football coach: he does not play for the team, but he trains them to run, block, and pass.

There is a cluster of cognate Greek words used in our passage. They are variations of the word *diakoneō,* which means "to serve." It is the word from which we get our word *deacon.* In our text, the words are first used to refer to the service or ministry of feeding widows. Later, they refer to the ministry of the Word of God. What is underscored by the words is that both tasks are ministries. Only later in the New Testament did they refer to the special office of deacon. Yet that development does not negate the more basic meaning.

We are all called to be ministers. Some feel that "the minister" is the preacher and "the ministry" is his profession. But growing churches cannot afford to think that way. If we do, the ministry becomes professional; it is taken away from the people. Christians then become "churchgoers" and little more.

A few years ago cardiopulmonary resuscitation (CPR) was unheard of outside the medical profession. Today, CPR is being taught on college campuses and through local fire departments, and even some businesses are training their workers in CPR. As a result, thousands of lives have been saved because laymen have learned how to serve in an emergency.

The church faces a similar emergency and cannot afford to leave its work to professionals.

Too often our churches are run by a philosophy of "mono-ministry." The pastor is to preach three sermons a week, do the visitation, write the bulletin, lead Sunday school, set up for worship, direct committees, and care for the needy. No wonder some pastors burn out! No wonder the average stay of a pastor in a church is three years!

Ministry is the responsibility of all God's people; it is not for professionals.

One church bulletin recently demonstrated its understanding of this point. After listing the names of the pastor, the assistant pastor, the organists, the elders, and the deacons, it then listed one more office. It said, "The Ministers—" Under that heading there were no names, only the words: "The Congregation."

The challenge of ministry is for every believer, and every believer must take up the challenge.

The Danger of Neglecting God's Word

There is a final danger that threatens growing churches. It is found in verses 2-7. That danger is neglecting the Word of God. The apostles say in 6:2: "It is not desirable for us to neglect the word of God in order to serve tables." Their primary call was "to prayer, and to the ministry of the word" (v. 4). To hinder a pastor from those two areas is to subvert the growth potential of the church.

Teaching and preaching the Word of God is essential. What gave birth to the throngs of people who joined the church? Preaching. What prompted the Jews to reach out to the Gentiles? Preaching. What brought forth the physical concerns for the needy? Preaching.

Paul writes in Romans 10:13, "Whoever will call upon the name of the Lord will be saved. How then shall they call upon Him in whom they have not believed? And how shall they believe in Him whom they have not heard? And how shall they hear without a preacher?"

When Paul wrote to Timothy, his personal disciple and fellow-worker, he said, "Until I come, give attention to the public reading of Scripture, to exhortation and teaching" (1 Timothy 4:13). In Ephesians, teaching is the means of equipping Christians to serve as the Body of Christ.

D. L. Moody said, "The best way to revive a church is to build a fire in the pulpit." Do you encourage your pastor by giving him the time for what he is called to do? Many churches require their pastor to make so many calls, attend so many board meetings, and be on so many committees that he does not have adequate time for the study of God's Word.

Just as the football coach trains his players to run, block, and pass, that same coach will also spend many hours preparing to teach his team. He studies the abilities of his players, looks at what the opposition might do, reviews the playbook, and designs new plays to teach to his team. He must prepare himself before he can teach others.

Paul also told Timothy to "pay close attention to yourself and to your teaching; persevere in these things; for as you do this you will insure salvation both for yourself and for those who hear you" (1 Timothy 4:16). Timothy's job was not to develop programs and serve on committees but to teach the Word.

How does a pastor build a fire in the pulpit? Paul told Timothy of two ways: First, pay close attention to your own life,

and second, pay attention to your teaching. Granted, that is difficult. Effective teaching and preaching involves more than just
transmitting information. To be effective, the message must travel through the transmitter. That takes energy. It is demanding
and time-consuming; but when the message permeates the man,
the man can communicate his message. For the pastor to teach
the Word, he must first have been taught by the Spirit.

Noted English Puritan Richard Baxter wrote of the demands
on pastors. He said that a pastor's temptations are greater than
those of most men, for the devil makes his sharpest attacks on
him. He said that the pastor's sins are more aggravated than most
men, because they have more hypocrisy in them; the honor of
Jesus and His truth is more at stake in pastors than in most men.
The souls of the body of Christ are dependent upon a pastor's
self-examination.

Can you begin to see the demands Scripture places on a
pastor-teacher? Can you see why the apostles would not neglect
the Word and prayer?

Another Puritan, John Owen, wrote, "In our prayers for our
people, God will teach us what we shall preach unto them."
Elsewhere he writes, "A minister may fill his pews, his communion roll and the mouths of the public, but when that minister is
on his knees in secret before God almighty, that he is, and no
more."

P. T. Forsyth said, "A preacher whose chief power is not in
studious prayer is, to that extent, a man who does not know his
business. Prayer is the minister's business. He cannot be a sound
preacher unless he is a priest."

The result of meeting these three dangers to a growing
church produced more growth than the apostles ever imagined.
Verse 7 says, "And the Word of God kept spreading; the number
of disciples continued to increase greatly in Jerusalem, and a
great many of the priests were becoming obedient to the faith."

Church growth can be short-lived, it can die out in a generation. But that was not the case for the church in Jerusalem, and
it need not be the case for us.

There will always be dangers confronting the Body of

Christ. But by the grace of God, may we listen and learn from the Word of God, which God has given to direct growing churches.

Remember

The mark of the Christian is divine love, and the manifestation of our love to the world is Christian unity.

Ministry is the responsibility of all God's people; it is not for professionals.

When the message permeates the individual, the individual can communicate the message. That is effective preaching.

"Prayer is the minister's business. He cannot be a sound preacher unless he is a priest" (P. T. Forsyth).

Questions

1. What are some types of discrimination found in the Christian church?
2. People in the early church felt that certain duties were not being fulfilled. What was their attitude toward such work?
3. Why is ministry the responsibility of all God's people?
4. What are the primary functions of the pastor according to Acts 6 and 1 Timothy?

Assignments

Discover ways in which you (and then your church) fall victim to each of the dangers inherent in church growth. Under God, determine positive steps that you can take to turn around dangerous situations.

Acts 7

Stephen and the System

> The world has yet to see what God can do with and for and through and in a man who is fully and wholly consecrated to Him.
>
> — Henry Varley

A few years ago, in a commencement address at Harvard University, Alexander Solzhenitsyn tried to summarize the root problem facing capitalism and Marxism. He said that the trouble with both systems is that men have forgotten God. One system does it by its materialist philosophy; the other system by its materialist economy.

But "the sin of forgetting God" is not just the sin of economics and governments. It can be the sin of religion as well. Religious people forget God by setting up a religious system in His place.

Stephen was up against such a system in Acts 7. Stephen charged that the religion of Jerusalem had turned bad. The supreme court of that city did not take Stephen's words lightly. They were furious. They tried to silence him by running him out of town, and finally they killed him by stoning. Stephan's hot piety was a threat to the council's cold religion.

A fire dies unless it is fed. The most natural thing in this world is for a person to lose his zeal, fervor, and drive. In the book of Revelation, John accuses the Ephesian Christians of having "left your first love" (Revelation 2:4).

Each of us forgets too soon. We all have the inherent tendency to drift from God.

The constant call of the Bible is to be on guard—to remember! Continually we are told to turn around, to repent, to draw near to God and submit to Him.

There are many ways to lose your first love, but Acts 7 focuses on one: ignoring God and putting religious substitutes in His place.

Stephen was on trial before the Sanhedrin. Witnesses, falsely testifying against him, said he spoke against the law and the Temple. In self-defense, Stephen offered a countercharge. He accused Israel of betraying God. He stated that they elevated the law and the Temple above God Himself and so fell into religious idolatry, wherein their religious system became an end in itself.

Stephen's charge was not new. In Isaiah 1 God denounced Israel's religious festivals and sacrifices as worthless worship, not motivated by love. In the gospels Jesus calls the Pharisees "whitewashed tombs" (Matthew 23:27). They had the fresh paint of religion on the outside, but inside they were full of the stench of hypocrisy and death.

Think of the church of Rome in the fifteenth century. It was trying to raise money by a system of indulgences. It offered a sacramental system that had become mechanical and that neglected personal faith.

Then God raised up men to reform the church and call it back to Scripture. One such man was Martin Luther. But sadly, those who followed men like Luther often let their faith harden into new systems—forms of Lutheranism that would rattle Martin Luther's bones, brands of Calvinism that would have caused uneasiness in Geneva.

It is not just a problem of the fifteenth and sixteenth centuries. We find it throughout church history: Franciscans who lost the zeal of Francis of Assisi; Jesuits who operated for different motives than that of Ignatius of Loyola; Methodists who grew too cold to preach the same warm gospel of John Wesley.

A similar temptation is faced at Moody Bible Institute. D. L. Moody loved Jesus. That is why he was driven to preach the gospel. But an institution in his name could easily become a system in itself. Only as Moody Bible Institute remains faithful to the love and goals of Mr. Moody's life can it truly be called the Moody Bible Institute.

Stephen faced a system that had grown cold. He faced it as a lover of Jesus, and he was tried, condemned, and murdered by that system. He stubbornly maintained his first love, and that made him a disturbing figure in his day. Like Isaiah, Luther, Francis, and Wesley, Stephen troubled the system because his life was open to God's Spirit.

There are many lessons in Acts 7, but give attention to three: Stephen's godliness, the system's ungodliness, and Stephen's defense.

STEPHEN'S GODLINESS

Stephen walked with God. The description provided in Acts 6-7 is short yet beautiful. The first thing presented is that he was selected as an assistant to the apostles. Along with six others, he was commissioned to care for widows in the Jerusalem church. The requirements for his job are given in Acts 6:3. Deacons must be men with a good reputation, full of the Spirit and of wisdom. Stephen was that kind of man.

But Stephen is further distinguished by his gift of preaching. He was so effective in serving that doors of ministry kept opening. That is still the way the Lord enlarges a person's ministry.

Another thing we learn about Stephen is that he was a "full" person. Acts 6:8 says that he was "full of grace and power." Further on, in verse 10, we are told that those who disputed with Stephen were unable to cope with the wisdom and the spirit of his speaking. That is because he was full of wisdom given by the Holy Spirit.

His godly character is revealed by his countenance. Twice we read that his face was aglow with the light of the Lord. In Acts 6:15 we read that Stephen's face was like the face of an angel.

Again, before his death, Stephen, full of the Holy Spirit, gazed into heaven. He saw the glory of God and Jesus standing at the right hand of God. It was as if he was so full of God that the stoning appeared to mean little.

Psalm 19 tells us that "the heavens declare the glory of God" (KJV*). At the end of the psalm, the servant, observing that revelation of heaven prays, "Let the words of my mouth and the meditations of my heart be acceptable in Thy sight, O Lord." The servant desires to join the heavens and declare God's glory. Like Mary, he has a soul that desires to magnify the Lord.

In Acts 7 God's servant Stephen declares the glory of God. His life magnified the reputation of God. Stephen's radiance was part of his witness. People just knew something was different. The moon sheds no light of its own, but merely reflects the light of the sun. That was Stephen. He claimed no glory for himself but displayed the glory of God. Yes, Stephen was a godly man.

STEPHEN FACED AN UNGODLY SYSTEM

The system in Acts 7 was so opposed to godliness that it attempted to stamp it out. The pages of history are filled with examples of people whose lives have been snuffed out by the system. The martyrs are prime examples. The irony of it all is that the system in Acts 7 was a religious one. But it had forgotten God. The people whom God chose as a nation were unfaithful.

Lest we forget the other ironies of history, we should remember that men acting in the name of the church have also shared this forgetfulness. The Museum of the History of Religion and Atheism in Leningrad does a thorough job of displaying all of the church's "dirty laundry" throughout history. Its purpose is to discredit the church as a fanatical institution of hatred. But we reply that such "dirty laundry" tells of a church that went bad, just like Israel. It forgot God and became a system unto itself. But that was not the true church. And what we find in Acts 7 is not the true Israel. It was apostate Israel.

The apostate religious system in Jerusalem was stacked against Stephen from the start. Men were secretly appointed to

*King James Version.

place false charges against him. The crowd was stirred so that it might approve of those who dragged Stephen away. And finally, false witnesses testified against him at the council. It was no trial but a mockery of justice. The system did not want truth, but self-protection, much like the trial of Jesus.

Two charges were laid against Stephen: He spoke against the law and the Temple. One of these charges was laid against Jesus too! In both cases, the intent of the accusers was plain. They were jealous of any threat to their religious territory.

What caused the system to go sour? Stephen's speech implies that the Israelites erred in trying to confine God. They tried to tame Him, disregard His laws, and limit His presence to a man-made Temple. If they could confine God to a building, then God's claim on human lives could be set aside. In short, men could control God. Religion was made manageable and self-serving. It sought to foster its own causes rather than the glory of God.

Was Stephen brash to disrupt the religious peace of Jerusalem? No more than Jesus or Paul. The harshest words in Scripture are aimed, not at those who have never heard the truth, but at those who have heard and then abandoned it.

Read the prophets who lambasted the corrupt institutions of Israel. Read Jesus' "woes" to the Pharisees in Matthew. Read Mark 12:24, where Jesus says to the Sadducees, "Is this not the reason that you are mistaken, that you do not understand the Scriptures, or the power of God?" Read Paul. His primary opposition was not the state, but those who held a form of godliness and denied its power. Paul told Timothy to avoid such men. Stephen was murdered by them—religious men who had forgotten God.

How can a church or a religious organization avoid falling into apostasy? Recently a leader of an evangelical missionary society commented on what seems to be the natural progression of organizations.

First, there is a godly man. He begins a mission or movement. Gradually they organize. The mission becomes a machine. And finally, when the man is gone, the machine becomes a monument.

How can that be avoided? Jesus' comments to the Sadducees are telling: they erred because they did not know the Scriptures—which witnessed to Christ—or the power of God.

Only as the individuals of a church or a para-church group
remain Christ-centered, and allow His spirit to shape their lives,
will the blood of their organization stay warm and alive. As
someone has said, "The main thing is to keep the main thing the
main thing."

STEPHEN'S DEFENSE

Stephen's defense can be wrapped up in two statements:
(1) God is greater than any religious system; and (2) God wants
a personal relationship with His people.

Acts 7 is an overview of Israel's history. It clearly establishes
the first point: God is greater than any religious system, even a
system that He has previously honored and blessed.

In Jesus' day the law and the Temple were key among Israel's institutions. They were pillars of the Jewish religion. Originally they were aids to preserve the covenant between God
and His people. But in time the law was obscured by rabbinic
traditions. The Temple became a national shrine, giving Israel a
false security that God would always be with them.

Not so, thundered Stephen. God, he said, is not bound to
this building. Nor is He bound to this land. The religious leaders
saw that as treason.

Then came Stephen's evidence. Consider Abraham: God
met with him apart from the Temple and outside of Palestine.
He called Abraham in Mesopotamia. What about Joseph? Although he was sold as a slave and sent to pagan Egypt, God was
with him. Then there was Moses. He was born in Egypt. Yet God
used him to deliver Israel. Even when he fled to Midian, God
revealed himself to Moses in a burning bush. When the children
of Israel wandered in the wilderness, God met His people in a
portable tent.

Where did things go wrong? Israel wanted to insure God's
presence by enshrining it. In so doing, they forfeited God's
blessing and power.

Then Stephen surprises us by saying that Solomon's Temple was wholly inadequate. Verse 48 reads, "The Most High does not dwell in houses made by human hands."

If God cannot be contained by a religious system, where then does He dwell? Stephen answers by quoting Isaiah. " 'Heaven is My throne, and earth is the footstool of My feet; what kind of house will you build for Me?' says the Lord."

The Sanhedrin quickly read the implications of Stephen's charge. If God is not here in our Temple, they thought, then our religion is a fraud. But now look at what happens. There is no search for truth but rather the quick impulse of self-preservation. Save the system! Silence the dissent!

But Stephen has one more point. Not only is God greater than religious systems, but more importantly, God wants a personal relationship with His people.

Already Stephen has pointed to men like Abraham, Moses, and Joseph as examples of true faith. But now, at the close of his speech, he points to the prophets and the Messiah as examples of true godliness. For Stephen, the godly man loves and obeys God. That is the essence of faith.

Stephen's words devastated his audience. Looking at his hardened accusers, he said,

> You men who are stiffnecked and uncircumcised in heart and ears are always resisting the Holy Spirit; you are doing just as your fathers did. Which one of the prophets did your fathers not persecute? And they killed those who had previously announced the coming of the Righteous One, whose betrayers and murderers you have now become. (vv. 51-52)

The religious elite of Jerusalem have become so corrupted, said Stephen, that they not only disobey God, but they stamp out true godliness. They kill those men who know God personally, just as they crucified Jesus.

Stephen's words had a tragic prophetic ring to them. For he too soon became the object of their violent antigodliness, and his life was cut down in an instant.

See what has happened here? The covenant hardened. Love

went cold. A relationship was replaced by a religious system. God was tied to a land and a building.

The church is not exempt from these threats. Too often our love hardens into a system. Our relationship with God becomes manageable and routine. Sometimes we confine God to a day—Sunday. Other times we confine Him to a building—the local church. Often we confine Him to a land—our own land or the West.

The first lesson we must learn is the one Stephen tried to teach the Sanhedrin: "The Most High does not dwell in houses [or structures, or systems] made by human hands" (v. 48). He is God, Maker of heaven and earth, Alpha and Omega. He is the One to whom every man shall one day give account.

The second lesson that Stephen preached, by his words and life, is that God wants a personal relationship with His people. He does not want a system or a dead religion. He wants you. He wants to be your God and your friend. He wants a partnership with His creatures. He wants them to love Him and enjoy Him forever.

This was the secret of Stephen's glory. Stephen was a man open to the Holy Spirit. Will you open your life to Him now? Do not resist God's Holy Spirit.

Remember

There are many ways to lose your first love, but Acts 7 focuses on one: ignoring God and putting religious substitutes in His place.

The moon sheds no light of its own; it only reflects the light of the sun.

God is greater than any religious system; and God wants a personal relationship with His people.

Questions

1. Describe the character of Stephen. What made him a good deacon?
2. How was Stephen's relationship with Christ obvious to those around him?

3. What was ironic about the system that killed Stephen?
4. Describe the process that led to the cold religion of Jerusalem's leaders. What is the cure for a system growing cold?
5. What is it that God looks for in His people?

Assignments

Compare your spiritual life to that of the Jewish leaders. Compare it to the life of Stephen. Determine whether you are listening to God's Spirit or resisting His Spirit.

Acts 8
Philip: A Model Witness

I determined that as I loved Christ, and as Christ loved souls, I would press Christ on the individual soul, so that none who were in the proper sphere of my individual responsibility or influence should lack the opportunity to trust and follow Christ. The resolve I made was, that whenever I was in such intimacy with a soul as to be justified in choosing my subject of conversation the theme of themes should have prominence between us, so that I might learn his need, and, if possible, meet it.

That decision has largely shaped my Christian life-work in the half-century that has followed its making.

—Henry Clay Trumbull

It is possible to be so tactful in our witness for Christ that we never make contact. The real question is not, Is this the best time for a personal witness for Christ? but rather, Am I willing to improve this time to witness for Christ? To Philip, the evangelist, God's call must have seemed strange. "Arise and go . . . to Gaza [a desert road]" (Acts 8:26). Philip had just concluded an overwhelmingly successful evangelistic campaign in Samaria. Many men and women were converted, and a great number were baptized in the name of Jesus Christ. Many were delivered of unclean spirits, the palsied and lame were healed, and joy abounded in Samaria.

Following that mighty moving of the Lord, Philip planned to continue his ministry in other Samaritan villages. But God directed him to the desert and to just one man.

Philip's experience outlines five principles about witnessing to others concerning Jesus Christ. Here we also see a picture of the sovereignty of God and His use of human instruments in reaching the lost. This story emphasizes the value God places on a single soul.

Philip was probably a Greek-speaking Jew, a deacon in the early church. God had given him a burden to reach the unbelievers beyond the borders of Judea, and he was likely the first to go outside the circle of Judaism to preach the gospel.

Philip had a heart so full that he had to share the gospel with the men and women in nearby Samaria. The full heart cannot be silent. One who has experienced a living faith will be strongly moved to share that faith.

This story indicates some of the ways in which God accomplished His sovereign purposes in reaching out in the early church so that believers were scattered abroad in many places (Acts 8:19). Men were trying to put out the light, and all they succeeded in doing was to spill and scatter the oil, and it flamed wherever it flowed. The apostles preached everywhere they went. Persecution only helped to spread the gospel.

A Successful Witness Is Obedient

At the peak of Philip's witnessing, the Lord told him to leave the city, the crowds, and the results and go down to Gaza, a desert place some eighty miles away. Verse 26 reads, "But an angel of the Lord spoke to Philip saying, 'Arise and go south to the road that descends from Jerusalem to Gaza.' "

Common sense would tell him to stay in Samaria, where he was having success, but the voice of God was clear. The Lord literally led Philip from the crowded city the barren desert, from the masses of people to a single soul. There is a lesson each of us must learn: God's ways are not always our ways.

Had Philip made a list of reasons for staying or for going, he would probably have stayed. It is necessary that we always obey the voice of God.

Philip's response to the Lord's command was immediate. Verse 27 reads, "And he arose and went." He had absolute trust in God that His orders were right. He did not argue, debate, discuss, or delay.

During a particular period in World War II, the North African campaign was seriously bogged down because a number of enlisted men had lost confidence in their officers. The resulting poor morale and poor fighting nearly proved to be disastrous.

It can be exactly that way with us. Not to act when God directs implies a lack of confidence in Him. We dare not hesitate to move when God speaks.

Philip's obedience is reminiscent of Abraham. God spoke to Abraham and said, "Take now your son, your only son, whom you love, Isaac, and go to the land of Moriah; and offer him there as a burnt offering" (Genesis 22:2). The command of the Lord seemed contrary to all God had promised. Isaac was the miracle child. Through him, all the promises of God would be realized. Yet in spite of all that, Abraham did not hesitate. He rose up early and obeyed God.

Be quick to obey the voice of the Lord. The opportunity may never present itself again, and a soul could be eternally lost.

A Successful Witness Recognizes That the Gospel Is for All Men

As Philip traveled toward Gaza, he came upon a caravan of soldiers and merchants, and in the center rode the treasurer of Ethiopia. Here was the man to whom Philip had been sent to share the gospel. Who was this person to whom God sent Philip?

He was probably a Gentile. We are told that the eunuch had just been to Jerusalem to worship. Some have suggested that he may have been a Jew who had reached a high place in the government of Ethiopia. Joseph, who became a ruler in Egypt, and Daniel, who reached a high position in Babylon, are examples of Jews who prospered in foreign lands. However, most Bible students believe that the man was a Gentile who had been converted to Judaism.

He was probably black. Always remember that the inclusive gospel cannot be shared by exclusive people. In Jesus Christ there is neither Jew nor Greek, bond nor free, male nor female.

The Body of Christ includes all races and the gospel is for every race. We cannot afford to discriminate in witnessing.

He was a statesman. He was involved in the government of a great country, a man of influence and great authority. Actually, he was in charge of the government's money and served as secretary of the treasury. That indicates that the gospel is not only for all races but for all levels of humanity—the up and out as well as the down and out.

He was religious. Scripture tells us that he "had come to Jerusalem to worship" (v. 27). The man recognized that he possessed a soul, and he went to great lengths to meet his spiritual needs. He was really a seeker of truth, and Philip found him reading the Old Testament prophecy of Isaiah.

No matter who we are, no matter where we have come from, the good news of the gospel is for all. If the early believers had confined their witnessing to their own people, it is likely that few of us today would know of Christ. God is no respecter of persons, and in our witnessing we should display the same openness.

A Successful Witness Shares His Faith with Enthusiasm

Philip had an inner fire. The Bible says he ran to meet the eunuch (Acts 8:30). Philip was a Spirit-led and Spirit-filled man in a hurry to do the will of God. Have you ever talked with a new mother about her baby? She becomes so excited she can hardly stop talking about the joy of her life. Philip was excited and anxious to speak of Christ.

Most of us need some heavenly enthusiasm. Abraham Lincoln said, "I like to see a man preach like he is fighting bees." The word *enthusiasm* really means "to be filled with God." If we are to enjoy successful witnessing, we need that heavenly fire. Opportunities are not forever.

A Successful Witness Knows the Scripture

The Bible account says, "And Philip opened his mouth, and beginning from this Scripture he preached Jesus to him" (v. 35). There are four interesting thoughts in verse 35.

Philip opened his mouth. Some of God's children rarely open their mouths to tell others of Christ. The Bible says, "Let the redeemed of the Lord say so" (Psalm 107:2). It is true that we witness by our lives, but our lips must express the gospel. Many followers of the cults live moral, upstanding lives. It is absolutely necessary for us to verbalize the reason why our lives are different from their exemplary way of living. The biblical combination is life and lip.

Philip began. Unfortunately, some people never do. They prepare to witness. They intend to witness. But they never begin.

Philip began at the same Scripture. Philip knew the Scriptures, and he knew how to use them. He identified Jesus as the Lamb Isaiah wrote about. He started where the man's interest was and moved on to point him to Christ.

Philip preached Jesus. I am sure that many other questions were asked and answered in their exchange. Evidently Philip took this man through the entire gospel story. He undoubtedly told him of Jesus' birth, His life, His teaching, His suffering, and His death for all. He must have told him of the resurrection and the new life offered in Jesus Christ, of the great commission, and of the importance of confessing Christ openly. Soon the Ethiopian was ready to make a life-changing decision.

However, let us not think that a lack of knowledge about Scripture should keep us from witnessing. A witness is one who tells what he has experienced. Lack of knowledge concerning the Bible's content does not change what has been experienced, but it should encourage us to study Scripture while continuing to witness.

A Successful Witness Seeks a Decision

As they approached a body of water, the Ethiopian said, "Look! Water! What prevents me from being baptized?" (v. 36).

How did he know about being baptized? Evidently Philip had presented the gospel so completely and convincingly that the Ethiopian was prepared to believe and be baptized. Philip answered, "If you believe . . . you may. And he answered and said, I believe that Jesus Christ is the Son of God" (v. 37). Upon hearing his confession, Philip baptized him.

He did not wait for the eunuch to gain a deep theological understanding of the gospel or to make a study of comparative religions. Philip knew a decision had to be made, and he gave him the opportunity.

The night of October 8, 1871, D. L. Moody was preaching in Chicago. He concluded his message by saying, "Go home and consider this week what to do with Christ. Next week come back and tell me what you decided."

That night, a fire destroyed most of Chicago, and that congregation never gathered again; some never saw the next sunrise. After that experience, Mr. Moody never again let people wait to make a decision.

Philip had witnessed effectively. The Ethiopian was changed by the power of the gospel. No doubt a new light was on his face, and a new thrill was in his spirit.

Philip had successfully witnessed concerning Jesus Christ, and a soul had been converted. In His divine plan, God has asked men and women to share the good news of salvation. He could have chosen to give the responsibility to His angels, or have created a special order of creatures who did nothing but witness to His love. But He gave mankind the privilege of sharing the gospel with fellow men; for it is only we who have experienced what Christ has done who can adequately share the difference He makes in a life. Determine to be like Philip—obedient to the Lord, warmhearted, and joyful, sharing with life and lip and seeking for a decision.

Remember

God's ways are not always our ways. It is necessary that we always obey the voice of God.

No matter who we are or where we come from, the good news of the gospel is for all people.

The biblical combination for witnessing is life and lip.

Following a clear presentation of the gospel, offer an opportunity to make a decision.

Questions

1. What resulted when the church underwent persecution?
2. Philip witnessed to the Ethiopian even though they were different types of people. What were the differences between the two?
3. Why is it important that we give a witness with our mouth and not just our life?
4. Why is it important that we offer people the opportunity to make a decision?

Assignment

Write out a one-page testimony of what Christ has done for you. Obtain a copy of a simple plan of salvation and begin to memorize it.

Acts 9
Paul: A Ray of Hope

When by the Spirit of God, I understood these words, "The just shall live by faith," I felt born again like a new man: I entered through the open doors into the very Paradise of God!

— Martin Luther

Have you ever been in a dark room and then were suddenly exposed to a brilliant light? Perhaps it was the light of the sun as you got up this morning. The effect was blinding. You were momentarily stunned. You probably closed your eyes or squinted to get used to the sun's powerful rays.

One day years ago, a man named Saul was walking along a darkened road. He was on his way to Damascus to harass Christians. But suddenly he found himself surrounded by an overwhelming light. It was stunning like the sun but even more so. It didn't blind him for a few seconds; it took him *three days* to recover his sight. Saul was shaken—so much so that the course of his life was changed.

Historian Will Durant said that Saul began the day "by attacking Christianity in the name of Judaism, and ended by rejecting Judaism in the name of Christ."

What was it that turned the bitter Saul into the apostle Paul? What changed him from a Christian persecutor into a Christian disciple?

In Acts 9 we find Saul in three different situations: in verses 1-2 we see Saul *without* the light; in verses 3-9 we see Saul *un-*

der the light, on the road to Damascus; and finally, in verses 10-31 we see Saul living *in* the light as he prepares for his ministry to the Gentiles. Let us consider these three phases of Saul's life.

SAUL WITHOUT THE LIGHT

The first two verses of the chapter portray Saul before Christ. What was he doing? He was breathing threats and murders against the disciples of Jesus.

You will remember that Saul's first appearance in Acts shows him standing with Stephen's murderers, holding their coats. His role in chapter 9 is far more aggressive. Now he is on the road to Damascus hoping to crush the Christian movement there. Chapter 22 says that Saul persecuted Christians to the death. He punished both men and women. Chapter 26 adds that he chased Christians even to foreign cities. When he found them, he forced them to blaspheme, brought them to punishment, and sometimes approved of their execution.

If there ever was a religious fanatic it was Saul. He lived according to the strictest sect of his religion. His model of religious purity was ancient Israel, which slaughtered its enemies in Canaan.

Perhaps a more contemporary example of violent religious zeal is seen today in the Middle East. Some years ago we read in our papers about the militant religious purges in Iran. Under Ayatollah Khomeini's direction, Islamic fundamentalists persecuted their enemies in a way that made the shah of Iran look like a decent man. Speaking of the persecution of infidels, Khomeini said, "Thanks to God, our young people are now . . . putting God's commandments into action. They know that to kill the unbelievers is one of man's greatest missions."

Why did Saul do it? Did God tell him to? No, there was no direct revelation as there was with ancient Israel. Rather, Saul saw his own violence as a service to God. Chapter 26 says that he hoped to obtain God's promise to Israel by his works. Saul's good work then, was to eradicate all religions that were contrary to the laws and traditions of Israel.

Yes, Saul was without the light of Jesus. He walked the road to Damascus in spiritual darkness. It was a dark road. His religion was based on human effort. He was spiritually blind. He left destruction in his wake. To him Jesus was a dead criminal and no more. Saul had no idea that each whipping he gave to Christians was a wound in the body of Christ. But how could he know, when his eyes were closed to the light of Jesus Christ?

SAUL UNDER THE LIGHT

If verses 1-2 show us Saul without the light, verses 3-9 describe Saul under the light.

Luke writes, "And it came about that as he journeyed, he was approaching Damascus, and suddenly a light from heaven flashed around him" (v. 3).

One secular historian tried to explain that by saying that Saul was fatigued from a long journey. The strength of the desert sun was too much for him. Perhaps a stroke of heat lightning lit the sky. It may have been Saul's frail epileptic body, or a mind tortured by doubt and guilt.

However, none of those explanations is sufficient. There is no trace of fatigue, heat lightning, or epilepsy in the text. And those would hardly explain the 180-degree turn in Saul's life.

What did Saul see? Saul saw the risen Christ. And that appearance was devastating. Under the light Saul fell to the ground. He was struck blind for three days, and he stopped eating and drinking.

The closest situation we have to this in the Bible, I believe, is the vision recorded in Isaiah 6. When Isaiah saw the Lord and heard the angels call "Holy, Holy, Holy, is the Lord of Hosts," he trembled. In anguish, Isaiah cried, "Woe is me, for I am ruined! I am a man of unclean lips, and I live among a people of unclean lips; for my eyes have seen the King, the Lord of Hosts" (Isaiah 6:3, 5).

Isaiah, with all his fine qualities, fell apart before the holiness of God. He saw his best as nothing before the Righteous One. And yet that was the prelude to his cleansing and commissioning as a prophet of God.

Saul was like Isaiah. He never really understood God until

God gave him a glimpse of His glory. And then Saul fell apart as a man. Only God could remake him.

Saul spent all his time trying to deny that Jesus was the Messiah. How could a man who was condemned by the high priest and who died a criminal's death be the Christ? That was not the way it was supposed to happen. But Saul knew differently when the voice of Jesus rang out saying, "Saul, Saul, why are you persecuting me? . . . I am Jesus whom you are persecuting" (vv. 3-4). Saul saw the risen Lord. He realized that he had been wrong. And now he looked to Jesus for a new beginning.

In that instant Saul became a new man. Even his name would change. All of his religion was not enough. Saul needed to see Christ and to trust in Him. That was the essence of his conversion. That is the story of Saul under the light. And it should be the story of every Christian under the light.

Am I saying that you have to have a dramatic Damascus road experience to be born again? Not at all. To some, conversion means swift change because of a vivid experience of having seen the Lord. But to many, it comes with a quiet yet firm confession in their hearts. The important thing is not the circumstances but act of trusting in Christ.

Are you a second-class Christian if you haven't had a dramatic conversion? Not at all. Perhaps you were raised by Christian parents. Then thank God for all the advantages that that brings. But if you are looking for drama, usually you only have to go back a generation or two to find it.

My own children can now look back on two generations of Christian parents. That is quite a heritage. But I have reminded them that if they want drama, they should consider their grandfather's conversion. He was not brought up under believing parents. He described his preconversion years as a wasted time of gambling, drinking, and soccer playing. He would place bets on athletic games and squander his savings. That got him into trouble and left his life empty. Then one day he went to a mission founded as a result of D. L. Moody's ministry in Glasgow. My dad gave his life to Christ, and he was never the same. When he came under the light of Christ he saw his sin for what it was. He confessed it and trusted Jesus.

SAUL IN THE LIGHT

So far we have seen how Saul once lived without the light of Christ. Then, on that dark Damascus road, he came under the light. Now we'll consider Saul's life in the light of Christ. This is seen in verses 10-31.

To say that Saul lived in the light is really to say that he was in Christ. Years later, Saul, better known as the apostle Paul, wrote to the Corinthians, "If any man is in Christ, he is a new creature" (2 Corinthians 5:17). That is exactly what we find in Acts 9. Saul is a new man. His mission, message, and character are different.

Consider first his mission. Saul went to Damascus with a strategy to smoke out Christians and then make them deny Christ. But when Saul arrived in that city he was ready to serve the same Lord that Christians served. In verse 15 Jesus says, "He is a chosen instrument of Mine, to bear My name before the Gentiles and kings and the sons of Israel." Saul was no longer the chief antagonist of the church. He was now its chief protagonist. He would travel throughout the ancient world proclaiming the gospel and building up the church. It is that mission that Saul is remembered for. Thus, the *Chambers Encyclopedia* says of Paul that "besides *his* achievements . . . the achievements of Alexander and Napoleon pale into insignificance."

Second, consider Saul's new message. He abandoned the traditions of the Pharisees and proclaimed that Jesus is the Son of God. That was a shocking confession for a former Pharisee. "Son of God" traditionally referred to the ideal king or the true Israelite. But now Saul applied it to Jesus. The long-awaited Messiah had come!

The Jews could not accept that. The trouble with Jesus, they said, is that He died a criminal's death on the cross. The Old Testament said that whoever died by crucifixion was accursed. Besides, the Messiah was expected to come as a triumphant liberator of Jerusalem.

But when Saul saw the risen Jesus, he knew better. He finally understood that Jesus' crucifixion had a purpose. He became a curse for us. He died in our place. He took our sin upon Himself. He gave us His righteousness. In that way Jesus became the Savior. He brought a liberation far more profound than the Pharisees had ever dreamed of. He brought a salvation that came not by works but by grace. That convinced Saul to give up trying to find favor with God. Instead he fixed his hope on the risen Lord.

Is that your message too? Have you looked to Jesus as your Savior? Or are you still on that dark road of Damascus trying to impress God by your service for Him? Saul saw that salvation was in Christ. He lived in that light.

Third, Saul not only had a new mission and message, but he had a new character. Living in the light of Christ will do that to you. It changes the real you. It gives you a new power to love God and a will to obey Him.

The *Encyclopaedia Britannica* describes Saul before his conversion as a bitter, intolerant, religious bigot. Yet after his conversion he is called a patient, kind, and self-sacrificing man.

Did all that happen in an instant? No! There is no such thing as instant godliness. True, there were some initial changes. Saul could now call a Christian man his brother and not his enemy. But much of Saul's character was forged in daily communion with God and in obedience to Christ. The crisis of salvation led to a process of obedience.

Galatians tells us that Saul spent three years in Arabia and Damascus shortly after his conversion. He did not dive into "Christian work" in Jerusalem until his faith had roots. Verse 23 alludes to that time. It was probably a period when Saul did the thinking and praying that equipped him to be an apostle. It gave him the spiritual backbone to launch out on three dangerous missionary journeys.

Time spent alone with Christ and suffering that came from obedience: those were the building blocks of Saul's character. What about yours?

Are you waiting for God to get in step with our "instant society" and manufacture for you some "instant godliness"? Then you will wait. God does not work that way. He wants your spiritual roots to grow deep, so that you can stand in all the storms of life. He wants you to be like the tree of Psalm 1—firmly planted by streams of water. He wants to teach you in the adventure of obedience.

It is not an easy road, but it is no dark road either. It is a road that is walked daily in the light of Christ.

What road are you on today? Are you on a dark road, like Saul, *without* the light of Christ? Then trust Him for your salvation. Are you *under* the light of Christ, as a young Christian, wondering where to go? Then make it your habit to trust and obey Him daily.

My hope is that you will live *in* the light and know all that God has for you—His mission for your life, His message for your life, and a character that comes from following the Lord Jesus Christ.

Remember

When Isaiah saw the Lord, he cried, "Woe is me, for I am ruined! Because I am a man of unclean lips, and I live among a people of unclean lips; for my eyes have seen the King, the Lord of Hosts" (Isaiah 6:5).

Conversion comes in many different ways, but the basic ingredients of repentance and faith are always there.

Paul wrote to the Corinthians, "If any man is in Christ, he is a new creature" (2 Corinthians 5:17).

Saul finally understood that Jesus' crucifixion had a purpose. He became a curse for us. He died in our place. He took our sin upon himself.

The crisis of salvation led to a process of obedience.

Questions

1. How does the fervor with which Saul persecuted Christians compare with his zeal for Christ following conversion?
2. Why was Jesus' death a stumbling block to Jews like Saul?
3. What pivotal fact about Jesus did Saul first recognize on the Damascus road?
4. After his conversion, what did Saul do to prepare himself for future Christian service?

Assignment

Consider the ways your life has changed since you stepped into the light of Jesus Christ. In what ways have you been obedient to the Great Commission to spread the light? Think about how you might make more effective use of opportunities to witness.

Acts 10
The Peace of God

Prejudice is the ink with which all history is written.
                                            — Mark Twain

Not long ago I was in a church in England. At the beginning of the service, the minister asked each one to give "the sign of peace" to one another. At this point, each leaned to the person next to him, shook his hand and said, "The peace of the Lord be with you." It was a beautiful gesture.

What an amazing resource Christians claim to have in a world torn apart by conflict and division. But is it just talk, or is there something to the claim? Was that minister engaged in wishful thinking? Or can we experience God's peace in a strife-torn world?

Each day news reports remind us that our world is woefully divided: Republicans against Democrats; our company against their company; management against employees; the CIA against the KGB; Iraq against Iran. In every area of life it boils down to "us" against "them." Our world desperately needs to experience peace. The account of Peter and Cornelius in Acts 10 gives ample evidence of the reality and attainability of the peace of God.

A major problem stood between Peter and Cornelius: one was a Gentile Roman soldier, the other a zealous messianic Jew. Yet both were marvelously drawn together. How did it happen? Look carefully at the two and discover who they were, what divided them, and how they resolved their differences. Through their story you will discover the healing peace of Jesus, which effectively restores hopeless relationships.

CORNELIUS'S CONCERN

Acts 10 opens with a description of Cornelius. We are told he was a Roman centurion assigned to Caesarea. Many soldiers discover their initial assignment to be quite unpleasant. They find themselves away from home, family, and friends, and in a strange environment. It is quite possible that that dislike was shared by Cornelius as well when he first undertook his military duties.

But Cornelius was no ordinary soldier. He had been observing the Jews. He saw their noble doctrine of Jehovah and the Messiah and became familiar with their sacred Scripture. He took the time to learn of their majestic worship. And after that careful study, something happened in his mind and heart. When Luke introduces us to Cornelius, he is already worshiping the God of Israel. He is on his search to find peace with God. Notice Acts 10:1-2: "Now there was a certain man at Caesarea named Cornelius, a centurion of what was called the Italian cohort, a devout man, and one who feared God with all his household, and gave many alms to the Jewish people, and prayed to God continually."

But there existed in Cornelius's life a conflict. As much as he loved the God of Israel, he was still a Gentile; he was born that way. Not only was he uncircumcised, but he had no desire to be circumcised as a grown man. According to the Jewish law, then, Cornelius was a second-class person. Life was less than kosher. He was totally influenced by his own Gentile culture, and that created a great barrier between Cornelius and Israel. Even though he sought for peace, complete peace eluded him.

Imagine the prejudice Cornelius felt every time he walked into the synagogue. Like the Temple, there were probably exclusive areas from which unclean Gentiles were prohibited from entry. In today's vernacular, they had to sit in the back of the bus.

How did Cornelius resolve the conflict? Verses 2-3 explain. First, there is no evidence that Cornelius was a complainer. That is the first resort of many church friends. If a problem comes up, they tell everyone about it but fail to tell the Lord.

Second, Cornelius did not leave the synagogue. That is often the second resort of church members. If it is not going our way, we leave and find another church.

Instead, Cornelius brought his problems to the Lord. Verse 2 says that he "prayed to God continually." That is what we find him doing at three o'clock in the afternoon.

Then suddenly, Luke writes, an angel of the Lord appeared to him in a vision. Cornelius froze! Reassuring him, the angel said, "Your prayers and alms have ascended as a memorial before God" (v. 4). The angel then commanded him to dispatch his men to Joppa. They were to search for a man called Peter, who would tell Cornelius how to find complete peace with God.

Not wasting any time, Cornelius obeyed. He called his men and sent them to find this man Peter. In fact, Cornelius went beyond mere obedience. He gathered his friends and relatives in expectant faith so that they could hear God's Word when Peter arrived.

Acts 10 presents Cornelius as a Gentile who loved the God of Israel, but who could not fully identify with the Jewish religion. He had not yet discovered the heart-settling peace for which he prayed and sought.

But do you notice how Cornelius began to solve his problem? He began with faithful prayer—then he obeyed what little God had revealed to him.

How do you respond to the conflicts of life? Do you get impatient and take matters into your own hands? Cornelius was an outsider who did it right, and God graciously responded to him by sending the gospel of peace through Peter.

PETER'S PROBLEM

Simon Peter—what do we know of him? By this time Peter had become a rather famous disciple. But like the other disciples, he still thought of himself as a Jewish Christian. In verse 9 we find Peter up on a roof praying. It may have been the only quiet place he could find.

Perhaps you can relate to Peter's prayer life. Remember Gethsemane? He fell asleep when he should have been praying.

Now we find him in the middle of his devotions, and he is distracted by a hungry stomach.

Yet just as God worked His purposes in Peter's garden nap, He now overrules in his rooftop prayers. Peter is given a vision that jars his convictions and causes him great theological difficulty.

What was the problem? In his vision, Peter saw a sheet descending from the sky, filled with all kinds of animals that he was forbidden to eat. It was a non-kosher smorgasbord.

Then suddenly God commanded him to kill the animals and eat them. Typically, Peter protested. "By no means, Lord, for I have never eaten anything unholy and unclean" (v. 14).

Peter's conflict was that he would not disobey the ritual laws of Israel. Three times he refused to obey God's new word. Then finally he realized that God was repealing some of the old laws for the sake of His people.

On the heels of that vision came another. By this time, Cornelius's servants were at Peter's door. They urged Peter to come and stay at their master's house and teach his family. Such a request was unthinkable for a Jew. The barrier between Jews, even Christian Jews, and Gentiles was great. Peter could never eat the unclean food at Cornelius's table. And Cornelius did not offer a vegetarian menu either.

But the Holy Spirit told Peter to go with them. God had prompted their visit in the first place. Hearing that, everything began to make sense for Peter. If Peter could eat the meat of animals and not defile himself, then a visit to Cornelius's home was no longer a problem.

Did you see how Peter began to work through his problem? His persistent prayer life made him receptive to God's new message. Before it, Peter was stumped. He had Christ's commission to fulfill, but he wondered how to convince Gentiles to accept Jewish circumcision. The answer came to Peter as he prayed. So often that is the time God chooses to speak a fresh word to His people. It was as true for Peter on the roof as it is for you at your bedside.

If Cornelius's prayer brought the gospel to the Gentiles,

then Peter's prayers removed the ancient barriers that would have prevented it. Look what happened.

Peter eventually arrived at Cornelius's home. There he preached the good news of Jesus Christ to this entire Gentile family.

At the onset of his sermon, Peter came to another startling conclusion. He exclaimed, "I most certainly understand now that God is not one to show partiality, but in every nation the man who fears Him and does what is right, is welcome to Him" (vv. 34-35). What a revelation!

Peter saw that peace through Jesus Christ was available not only to Jews but to all men. So he baptized his audience when they received his message. Then he welcomed them into full membership of God's family. The peace of the Lord was indeed with Peter and Cornelius that day. It was only God's peace that could break through the mighty barriers of culture and religion. It is only the peace of Jesus that can heal your broken situation.

Sometimes we bicker and bargain, trying to hammer out our difficulties. Broken pieces are inevitable. It is only when we look to God through His Son that God's heat warms us and we become pliable.

Think of your relationship as a triangle. God is at the top. You and your rival are at each bottom corner. If you first try to approach each other, you necessarily leave God out. And when conflicts arise, there you are, head-to-head like rams. Horns lock. Bruises abound.

But another way exists. The alternative is first to draw near to God. That opens the route to peace. When we come to God and pray for His peace, we find ourselves drawn toward unity at the top of the triangle.

That is why it is important for husbands and wives to pray together regularly. Worship is important in the home. Church factions can be reunited. As we kneel together before the Triune God, we find ourselves on equal footing.

Sixty-two years ago, after a bitter First World War, two European families emigrated to America. One family came from Scotland. The husband had fought for Britain in the trenches of Belgium. The other family was German. Herr Schnell fought under the Kaiser. Entering the New York harbor by boat, they passed a great statue that welcomed them with the promise of peace—the Statue of Liberty.

At the base of that statue appears the following inscription: "Give me your tired, your poor, your huddled masses yearning to breathe free: the wretched refuse of your teeming shore. Send me the homeless, tempest-tossed to me. I lift my lamp beside the golden door." There was a promise to bring tired rivals together as citizens of a new nation. Those immigrants were the grandparents of our four children.

The words of that statue are words similar to those that Christ would have you hear today: "Give me your factions and disputes, your broken marriage and bitter heart. Give me your prejudices and stubborn spirit. Send these to me, and I will lift my lamp beside the golden door."

Cornelius and Peter discovered that the peace of the Lord is no relic or fantasy. It is a living peace that Christ offers, and it remains available to you today.

Give Jesus your toughest conflict. Look to Him in faith. And may the peace of God be with you today and forever.

Remember

According to the Jewish law, Cornelius was a second-class person. His peace, therefore, was incomplete.

Cornelius wasted no time in obedience. In fact, he went beyond mere obedience in gathering his friends and relatives in expectant faith so they could hear God's Word when Peter arrived.

After presenting his problem before God, Cornelius obeyed what little God had revealed to him.

Often it is while we are praying that God chooses to speak a fresh word to His people.

Peter concluded, "I most certainly understand now that God is not one to show partiality, but in every nation the man who fears Him, and does what is right, is welcome to Him" (vv. 34-35).

Broken pieces are inevitable. It is only when we look to God through His Son that God's heat melts us, and we become pliable.

The living peace offered to Cornelius and Peter is available for healing broken relationships today.

Questions

1. Describe the character of Cornelius. What type of a man was he?
2. What made Cornelius different from other Roman soldiers occupying Israel?
3. How did Cornelius deal with his problem?
4. What was the conflict Peter felt, and how was it resolved?
5. What conclusion did Peter come to? How did it alter the course of history?
6. Describe how a triangular relationship illustrates the proper way to heal relationships.

Assignment

Identify areas of conflict that you may have with others. Make those conflicts a matter of prayer, seeking God's guidance in overcoming the problems. Then take immediate action as God directs.

Acts 11
A Tale of Two Churches

The (Early) Church was not an organization merely, not a movement, but a walking incarnation of spiritual energy. The Church began in power, moved in power and moved just as long as she had power. When she no longer had power she dug in for safety and sought to conserve her gains. But her blessings were like the manna: when they tried to keep it overnight it bred worms and stank.

— A. W. Tozer

The earliest church in Jerusalem was beset with problems. Sure, there had been growth. But there were also problems. It was a human church, so it was really not that different from today's churches.

Already in our study of Acts we have found hypocrites and cheats such as Ananias and Sapphira. There was also the jealousy of the Greeks in chapter 6, and a man named Simon who tried to buy his way into the Christian life. Put the myths aside: the Jerusalem church was not as problem-free as we sometimes imagine. They faced difficulties like churches do today..

What stands out about this church is not the problems, but the way in which God worked through those problems. Each problem became an opportunity for growth.

Chapter 11 relates a tale of two churches. One church was the older, mother church of Jerusalem. The other was the younger, daughter church of Antioch. The first gave birth to the second. And as in every birth, there are moments of intense pain. That pain became a means to a great end: bringing the gospel of Christ to the Gentiles.

In chapter 11 we discover four problems faced by the Jerusalem church. Like present-day church problems, each of them, seen in the light of God's sovereign will, offered great opportunities for church growth.

THE PROBLEM OF PERSECUTION

First, there was the problem of persecution. Verse 19 tells us that "those who were scattered because of the persecution that arose in connection with Stephen made their way to Phoenicia and Cyprus and Antioch."

You may remember the story. An outbreak of violence against the church followed Stephen's murder, and Christians fled from Jerusalem. Can you imagine how that must have discouraged the believers there? Jesus left them with a Great Commission, and now their base of operations was destroyed. They fled to places where there was no Christian witness. They were fugitives on the run. Some were beaten, some killed. It seemed as if all the work that had been accomplished in Jerusalem thus far had been wasted.

But there was another side to the tragic string of events. Paul wrote that "God causes all things to work together for good to those who love God" (Romans 8:28). All things? Even flogging? Even what appeared to be the worst of times? Yes, all things.

We face a profound mystery here. From a human perspective, things look bleak. It seemed as if evil was triumphing. But as Christians we maintain that God carries out His purposes in history. The mystery comes in holding the two things together: the sovereignty of God and the deeds for which only men can be responsible.

A little boy took the train from London to Edinburgh to visit relatives. He was seated in the front of the train with his parents but did not want to take the trip at all. As the train pulled out of the London station, he escaped his parents' watch and ran toward the back of the train in an assertion of his will. Yet even though he was bent on going in another direction, he was on a train for Scotland. All the running in the world would not stop him from getting there.

So it is with men who carry out evil deeds. Even though they try to disrupt God's rule, it is God's will that wins the day.

To say that God was providentially involved in the Jerusalem persecution may sound harsh. It may cause you to react defensively, as when someone suggests that God worked through the communist purges in Cambodia and Vietnam, causing many refugees to come to Christ as they escaped. Of course there is truth to that. But fanatical governments choose their own actions. It is wrong to ascribe such evil to God. What we can say is that in God's will all things work together for good to those who love God.

Acts 11 tells us that Stephen's murder preceded a great gospel outreach. At first all looked grim. Christians were martyred and persecuted. But the bloodshed and scattering, by God's grace, were turned into a triumph of the gospel. The dispersion of believers forced a missionary endeavor.

So we can rightly condemn Stephen's murderers for their evil deeds. Nevertheless, we can rejoice that his death had redemptive meaning. It led to the founding of one of the most dynamic churches in the ancient world—the church of Antioch.

Just as with the violent crucifixion of Jesus, evil raged but did not triumph. God transformed injustice and agony into a victory of grace. A great problem for the church became an outstanding opportunity to further the cause of Christ. The door was open that led to a mission among the Gentiles.

THE PROBLEM OF EXCLUSIVISM

A second problem was that of exclusivism. Jewish Christians were culturally biased against the Gentiles. You will recall that Gentiles were considered unclean. The way to win them, conventional wisdom said, was to get them circumcised as Jewish Christians. The road to Christ led through Jerusalem. That is why Peter was criticized when he returned from his visit to Cornelius. The Jews in Jerusalem thought he had defiled himself.

The great question facing the Jerusalem church was: Can a Gentile come to Christ without becoming a Jew? Can the synagogue and circumcision be bypassed? Traditional Christianity in Jerusalem said no. Then Peter challenged that wisdom. He said that God had given him a new revelation. He had seen Gentiles receive the same Lord, the same Spirit, and the same gifts as the Jews, only without the trappings of Jerusalem. In response to that he cried, "Who was I that I could stand in God's way?" (v. 17).

The Christians in Jerusalem became exclusivists because they closely tied the gospel to Jewish cultural and religious forms. They froze the gospel in their tradition.

That was not just a Jewish temptation. It is a trap that the church has fallen into time and again. We preserve the form that the gospel comes in when it enters our culture. Then as we preach to other cultures we give them both Christ and our cultural forms. Western missionaries have sometimes been criticized for sharing a westernized Christ.

There is difficulty in pointing fingers here. The Jerusalem church promoted Jewish Christianity. But look what happened.

Did the Greeks learn the lesson? No! The Greeks preached the gospel in Greek terms, often using ideas borrowed from their philosophers.

Then there was the Roman church. It understood the gospel in Latin forms. The reformers tried to correct that, but the gospel was influenced by their culture as well. Presbyterians proclaim a gospel colored by Geneva and Edinburgh; Lutherans, a gospel flavored by Wittenburg. In America our call for faith and repentance is sometimes related to the American Dream.

The problem is one of containing new wine in old wineskins. When Paul told Timothy that the Word of God is not bound, he meant that it could not be confined by anything, including cultural forms. Perhaps that is why Paul said he became all things to all people.

The gospel works through cultures. It worked through Jerusalem. Then it came to a new culture in Syria, to a city called Antioch. It passed through the Greek cultures of Asia minor, on to Rome, northern Europe, and the Americas. Now it is making great headway in the Orient.

What kind of wineskins do you place the gospel in? Would your church have clung stubbornly to the traditions of Jerusalem?

Thank God that the problem of cultural exclusivism was overcome. Thank God that the gospel did come to Antioch, the second city of the early church. For had it not come to Antioch, it would never have made it to your city.

THE PROBLEM OF SURPLUS OF LEADERSHIP

A third problem facing the Jerusalem church may surprise you. Perhaps the best way to describe it is to say that they were organizationally top-heavy. There were too many chiefs and not enough Indians. They were overstaffed.

All the disciples and all the apostles of Jesus since Pentecost were in Jerusalem. There was a concentration of gifted people in one city. Can you imagine what the Moody Bible Institute would be like if all of its graduates for the past one hundred years remained on the Chicago campus? The city would have more evangelists, translators, pilots, youth workers, and pastors than it could handle. They would be stepping on each other's toes and not attending to the work of God.

Luis Palau once likened a large cluster of Christians to a farmer's supply of cow manure. When it all remains in one place, not much good is accomplished and the aroma is overwhelming. Only when the fertilizer is spread around does it begin to do good.

There were too many trained Christian leaders piled up in Jerusalem. Once they began to move out into Samaria and the uttermost parts of the earth great things began to happen.

It all began when those who were scattered because of Stephen's death took risks to share the gospel. Gentiles responded immediately. News filtered back to Jerusalem that God was performing a mighty work among the Gentiles in Antioch. What happened? Rather than get jealous of a new church, the elders sent some of its best men to Antioch to help out.

First came Barnabas, a perfect choice for a Gentile mission. He was raised in a Gentile environment and understood their way of life. Next came Saul. Barnabas sent for him, and they each gave an entire year to teach the new Christians what it meant to be disciples of Jesus. Finally, the Jerusalem church sent prophets like Agabus. The mother church gave some of its best men to the new work in Antioch.

What about your congregation? Perhaps the church in America can be likened to the Jerusalem church. We are organizationally top-heavy. We are overstaffed. Compared to the rest of the world, we have many people who claim to be born again. In relation to other countries, we have large numbers of Bible schools and seminaries that are full. Unlike most nations, we have expertise in communications technology and unparalleled wealth in our churches. We have all the tools: people, money, and training. Yet, like the Jerusalem church, we are here in one place while the world cries out for the good news.

What are you doing with your training? Whom are you sending out as a church? Whom do you support with your offerings?

After the Battle of Britain, Winston Churchill said, "Never in the field of human conflict was so much owed by so many to so few." Compared to the billions of people on our globe, the American church is small. But in the commission to send out the gospel it is the few who owe much to the many.

When Churchill rallied his countrymen to that significant battle he said, "Let us brace ourselves to our duties and so bear ourselves that, if the British empire and its commonwealth last for a thousand years, men will say, 'This was their finest hour.' "

This could be the church's finest hour if she were to use the tools and opportunities that God has given to her. By God's grace, may we brace ourselves for our duties and finish the task.

THE PROBLEM OF FAMINE

A fourth problem facing the Jerusalem church was famine. When famine came to Judea, the church was not prepared. They simply did not have the resources to cope. But things were different in Antioch. For some reason, they had a surplus of funds when hard times hit. What did they do? Rather than making themselves more comfortable, they sent relief aid to the mother church. Verse 29 reads, "And in the proportion that any of the disciples had means, each of them determined to send a contribution for the relief of the brethren living in Judea." Evidently, the Jerusalem church had trained its daughter well. When the Antioch believers saw other Christians suffering, they responded with generosity. The giving now went both ways. There was interdependence, a Body life. Jerusalem had given of its riches to Antioch, and now the church in Antioch responded in kind. What a striking lesson in stewardship!

Sometimes our churches are isolated, out of touch with the needs of Christians elsewhere. There are churches in the suburbs that probably come into little contact with the overt physical need in the cities. In Antioch the Christians kept in touch with churches that were needy. In a sense, they were "world Christians," committed to church involvement in other parts of the world. That was especially true once they began sending out missionaries to Asia Minor.

There are all kinds of ways in which our churches can give like the Antioch Christians. Your church might establish ties with a church in the third world. You might venture into the inner city and commit yourself to a church there. No matter where you are located, you have at least two things in common with the churches of Jerusalem and Antioch. First, you have been given gifts and resources with which to minister. And second, there are still needy churches all over the world.

Did you remember that it was in Antioch that the disciples were first called "Christians"? Originally, it was an insulting nickname. The word really means "servants or slaves of Christ." What an appropriate name for a young church that responded generously to the needy. What a fitting title for people who faced problems in the church with a steady trust in Christ. They were servants of Jesus. What about your church? How "Christian" are you? Do you live up to the name?

It is said that Alexander the Great allowed some of his soldiers to bear his name; but if one of them conducted himself dishonorably or timidly, Alexander would say, "Change your name or mend your manners." So too, no church that is selfish or exclusive has the right to bear the name of its selfless Lord. He is the Lord of the church. Let us be steadfast in being His servants. Let us live up to His name in all the problems that confront us as His people.

Remember

God still carries out His purposes in history. The mystery comes in holding these two things together: the sovereignty of God and the deeds for which only man can be responsible.

The Christians in Jerusalem became exclusivists because they closely tied the gospel to their culture and religious forms.

The mother church gave some of its best men to the new work in Antioch.

This could be the church's finest hour if she were to use the tools and opportunities that God has given to her.

No church that is selfish or exclusive has the right to bear the name of its selfless Lord.

Questions

1. What characterized the situation following the death of Stephen?
2. Describe the problem of exclusivism and how it affected the Jerusalem church.
3. Why can surplus leadership be dangerous?
4. Describe what your church has in common with both the Jerusalem church and the church at Antioch.

Assignment

Does your church fit the title "Christian" as did the one in Antioch? Determine how you can help it to rightly be called a Christian church. In what areas of your personal life do you not live up to the name "Christian"? Identify ways that can be changed.

Acts 12
Prayer Changes Things

The principal cause of my leanness and unfruitfulness is ow-
ing to an unaccountable backwardness to pray. I can write or
read or converse or hear with a ready heart; but prayer is
more spiritual and inward than any of these, and the more
spiritual any duty is the more my carnal heart is apt to start
from it.

— Richard Newton

During World War II Captain Eddie Rickenbacker and Ser-
geant Johnny Bartek drifted in a rubber raft for many days.
Johnny Bartek writes:

We realized we were in no condition to expect help from
God. We spent many hours of each day confessing our sins to
one another and to God. Then we prayed, and God answered.
It was real! We needed water. We prayed for water and we got
water—all we needed! Then we asked for fish, and we got
fish. And we got meat when we prayed. Sea gulls don't go
around sitting on people's heads waiting to be caught! On that
eleventh day when those planes flew by, we all cried like ba-
bies. It was then I prayed again to God and said: "If you'll send
that one plane back for us, I promise I'll believe in You and
tell everyone else." That plane came back and the others flew
on. Some would say "It just happened." It did not! God sent
that plane back! (*Autobiography of an American Hero* [Engle-
wood Cliffs, N.J.: Prentice-Hall])

Prayer does change things. The account of a prison escape

in Acts 12 illustrates that fact and teaches us some important concepts about prayer.

After the conversion of Saul of Tarsus, the followers of Jesus enjoyed a time of rest. But it did not last long.

Herod Agrippa, the first grandson of Herod the Great, began to persecute the church. It was the fifth persecution recorded by Luke against the infant church. Herod was a patron of the Jewish faith and worked hard at keeping the favor of the people he ruled. Verse 2 records one means by which he did this: "He had James the brother of John put to death with a sword."

James was the son of Zebedee, an older brother of John. Together with Peter, the three had become the inner circle of the twelve disciples. The three were the only ones present at the raising of Jairus's daughter and the transfiguration of Jesus, and were the closest to Jesus when He agonized in the garden of Gethsemane. But James was killed by the sword.

That evil act appeared to please the people, and so Herod proceeded to "arrest Peter also" (v. 3). Quickly Peter was arrested, jailed, and carefully guarded.

THE CHURCH AT PRAYER

Verse 5 reads, "Prayer for him was being made fervently by the church to God."

Alfred Tennyson wrote, "More things are wrought by prayer than this world dreams of." That is true. In fact, prayer is stronger than chains and iron gates, as Acts 12 reveals. No power on earth can even faintly compare with prayer power. Today we need to cultivate persevering prayer.

Take note of what the gifted Martin Luther had to say about the power of prayer: "I judge that my prayer is more than the devil himself. If it were otherwise, I would not have fared as well. Yet men will not see and acknowledge the great wonders and miracles God works on my behalf. If I should neglect to pray but a single day, I should lose a great deal of the fire of faith." Do you neglect prayer? If Jesus, the sinless Son of God, found it necessary to spend time in prayer, we as sinful creatures should find prayer indispensable.

A Christian student once commented, "I have only missed

my prayer time once or twice this term. . . . I can easily believe
that it is next in importance to accepting Christ. For I know that
when I don't spend time in prayer, things go wrong." Prayer is
the gymnasium of the soul.

The entire church, frightened and stunned by the murder
of James, turned to unceasing prayer for Peter. Often when confronted with difficulties, the response is, "Well, at least we can
pray about it." We often place prayer low on our priority list or
see it as a last resort to be used when we are unable to think of
anything else to do. In reality, prayer should be our first response to problems. Then, through that prayer, we should seek
guidance for the steps we would take.

The prayer of the church in Jerusalem became intense and
insistent. There was no letup.

Prayer is a gracious privilege but also a sacred responsibility. The neglect of prayer constitutes disobedience to God. What
is your response to difficulties?

GOD'S ANSWER TO PRAYER

Carefully observe verses 6-10:

> And on the very night when Herod was about to bring him
> forward, Peter was sleeping between two soldiers, bound with
> two chains; and guards in front of the door were watching
> over the prison. And behold, an angel of the Lord suddenly
> appeared, and a light shone in the cell; and he struck Peter's
> side and roused him, saying, "Get up quickly." And his chains
> fell off his hands. And the angel said to him, "Gird yourself
> and put on your sandals." And he did so. And he said to him,
> "Wrap your cloak around you and follow me." And he went
> out and continued to follow, and he did not know that what
> was being done by the angel was real, but thought he was
> seeing a vision. And when they had passed the first and sec-
> ond guard, they came to the iron gate that leads into the city,
> which opened for them by itself; and they went out along one
> street; and immediately the angel departed from him.

Peter's situation appeared to be hopeless. He was in prison
(v. 4) bound by two chains between two soldiers (v. 6). Between
Peter and the street were two separate guard stations and the

main iron gate separating the prison compound from the street.

Stories coming out of prisoner of war camps in Germany tell of many plans for escaping. A recent newspaper story explained how special games of Monopoly were developed and supplied to POWs. Hidden inside the game boards were maps showing safe escape routes. Bundles of Monopoly money actually concealed documents and real money needed by escaping prisoners.

Such elaborate schemes are not needed by God. God's resources are limitless. He has no need for pills or needles to put people to sleep. Nor does He need keys, hacksaws, blowtorches, or Monopoly games to release people from prison. He has millions of angels anxious to obey His slightest bidding. God's angels are as swift as the wind and like a flaming fire. Those angels are sent out to minister to each believer (Hebrews 1:7, 14).

It is intriguing to notice that the angels took care of many things for Peter, like waking him up and releasing him from his chains; but God does not do for us what we can do for ourselves. Verse 8 says, "Gird yourself and put on your sandals." God often answers prayer by showing us what we can do for ourselves while He cares for the things beyond us. Prayer should never become a substitute for work.

In addition, the answer did not come until the very last moment. Also, in verse 10 the angel accompanies Peter for one block and then leaves. This seems to say, "Peter, you are on your own." Prayer does not relieve us of our God-given sense.

THE RESULTS OF PRAYER

Peter was released from jail. Of course that was the first and foremost result. God miraculously delivered Peter from jail and potential death. At first he thought his release was a dream (v. 9), but he soon realized the experience was real and he was free (v. 11).

Circumstances may look impossible to man. But never forget that our God's control of the universe goes so far beyond our situation that circumstances pale next to the answers He gives our prayers.

The church was astonished. Verse 16 says, "But Peter continued knocking; and when they had opened the door, they saw him and were amazed."

That's quite an indictment on their faith and prayers. Verses 13-16 relate how Peter came and knocked at the door. A young girl named Rhoda answered the knocking. But even before she opened the door, Rhoda recognized Peter's voice and rushed back to the prayer meeting shouting, "Peter's at the door!"

Someone said, "Rhoda, you've gone mad!" Someone else concluded, "They have killed Peter, and it's his spirit at the door." Then verse 17 describes how Peter calmed them down and described how the Lord had led him out of prison.

How often we lay requests before God yet fail to recognize the answers when He sends it.

The soldiers were frightened. Verse 18 reads, "Now when the day came, there was no small disturbance among the soldiers as to what could have become of Peter."

God had been at work, the prayers were answered, and Peter was free. Yet the unbelievers were shaking in their boots. They failed to comprehend what had happened. They were confused, and it resulted in fear.

Remember the Philippian jailer in Acts 16. When the earthquake opened the prison doors he assumed the prisoners had escaped. Knowing he would have to pay with his own life if they had, he prepared to kill himself. That same fear, on top of the confusion, came upon those guarding Peter. When God answers prayers, the world is left wondering about its own safety and frightened at the power of God.

Herod thought he could mock God. He was anxious to please the people. He was out to cater to them, and so he killed James, and he intended to do away with Peter; but God had other plans. Herod was smitten dead. Verses 21-22 tell about it: "And on an appointed day Herod, having put on his royal apparel, took his seat on the rostrum and began delivering an address to them. And the people kept crying out, 'The voice of a god and not of a man!'" When Herod received that tribute, Scripture says, "And immediately an angel of the Lord struck him because he did not give God the glory, and he was eaten by worms and died" (v. 23).

The answers God gives sometimes far surpass the requests

of mankind. In the midst of the persecution by Herod, Peter was thrown into prison. The church in Jerusalem fervently prayed for him (v. 5). God not only brought about the release of the apostle, but, going beyond what the believers had prayed for, He brought to an end the very source of the difficulty.

Oh, yes, all this came in answer to the prayers of the church. Prayer changes people, and prayer changes circumstances. It taps into the very power of God and bids Him to act in our midst.

Remember

"More things are wrought by prayer than this world dreams of" (Alfred Tennyson).

"If I should neglect prayer but a single day, I should lose a great deal of the fire of faith" (Martin Luther).

The greater the trial, the greater the triumph.

God does not do for us what we can do for ourselves.

Prayer is not to relieve us of our God-given sense.

Prayer changes people, and prayer changes circumstances.

Questions

1. Set the stage for Peter's being placed in prison. Using a Bible dictionary, find out something of the character of Herod and the type of family he came from.
2. Summarize the importance of prayer in a believer's life.
3. What was Peter's responsibility in his escape? What was the angel's? How do the two relate?
4. Why do you think the church did not expect Peter to show up at their door?

Assignment

Involve yourself in an active prayer ministry: join a prayer group or chain, begin praying for specific missionaries and their mission organizations, and ask your pastor for specific ways you can pray for him and your church.

Acts 13
The First Missionary Journey

> The Spirit of Christ is the spirit of missions, and the nearer
> we get to Him the more intensely missionary we must be-
> come.
>
> — Henry Martyn

To liberal journalists, to some modern theologians, and to
many secular people, the term *missionary* is an unpopular
word. It stirs up images of people in khaki attire carving their
way through the jungle with a machete and Bible, ready to impose their morality on noble savages. There are charges that the
William Careys, the Hudson Taylors, and the David Livingstones
were really spiritual colonialists. But most of all, the missionary
is criticized for his audacity to enter another culture with the
claim that he has the truth. It is his truth-claim that is most offensive to the modern mind.

A British theologian has registered this complaint: "There
has been too much thought of gaining converts, of winning the
world, of expanding the church." What is important, he says, is
self-giving. That should be the essence of missionary activity. In
his words, self-giving "may well [be given] without . . . explicitly
confessing the Christian faith." In other words, he calls for sharing the life of Christ without the name of Christ.

The best way to respond to such theology is to point to the
Bible itself. Can you imagine Israel being a light to the nations
without talking about Jehovah or His law? Can you imagine Jesus
sending out His disciples, telling them to do good deeds, with-

out mentioning the good news of the gospel itself? It is inconceivable.

When evangelicals are criticized for an exclusive missionary message, they are criticized for being Christian, for following the example of the Lord Jesus and His disciples. At the end of Matthew Jesus tells His followers, "Make disciples of all the nations, baptizing them in the name of the Father and the Son and the Holy Spirit, teaching them to observe all that I commanded you" (Matthew 28:19-20).

In Acts 13 we read about the first missionary journey of the early church. It comes as no surprise to see Saul, now known as Paul, and Barnabas entering Asia Minor with the goal of winning converts and reaching the world for Christ. This first journey was a modest one, yet it bore great fruit. For in less than three hundred years the emperor himself would declare the teaching of Christ as the official religion of Rome.

Let us look at this first missionary journey in some detail. The chapter divides easily into three parts: their commission, their power, and their message.

THEIR COMMISSION

Verses 1-3 are full of useful information for any church interested in evangelism.

Keep in mind that the young church at Antioch was just getting its feet on the ground. Paul and Barnabas had been there for about a year.

Two offices are mentioned, those of prophet and teacher. We have here an early, simple form of church government. But notice that leadership is shared among five men. A year before, that probably was not the case. There were only two—Paul and Barnabas.

Evidently those two disciples trained others to do the work. They literally worked themselves out of a job. Paul's teaching elsewhere affirms that pattern of church leadership. In Ephesians, He recommends that teachers equip others to do the work of the ministry. Paul's theology was not decorative; it was lived, tested, and shared.

Notice the makeup of the leadership. No affirmative action programs existed in Paul's day. No Roman regulations required the hiring of minorities. But clearly a multicultural staff existed. Barnabas came from Cyprus. Simeon probably immigrated from Africa. So did Lucius. Paul, of course, was from Tarsus. Perhaps only Manaen was a native of the cosmopolitan city of Antioch. So let us set the record straight: the early church was inclusive. There was no partiality in Jesus Christ.

Paul conducted three missionary journeys, but they were not all laid out for him from the beginning on some grand blueprint. Each developed day-by-day as a journey of faith.

Verse 3 presents the Antioch church in the midst of worship when the Holy Spirit calls Paul and Barnabas. Here we find another example in the book of Acts that illustrates the power of prayer. The Holy Spirit often speaks while we are in prayer. And He clearly spoke to those disciples, saying, "Set apart for Me Barnabas and Saul for the work to which I have called them" (v. 2).

Another aspect of the Antioch Christians was their fasting. That provides guidance for any Christian in the midst of decision-making. As the Holy Spirit spoke, the men fasted and prayed. They gave themselves wholly to the Lord so that they might be certain that they heard His voice and not the voice of selfish ambition.

I recall some of the major decisions in my own life. Whenever I sensed the call of God, I would block out a large portion of time to pray. Often I would check into a hotel room where there were no phone interruptions. My wife would not tell anyone where I was. I would wait on the Lord and search my own heart to see if God was prompting me to move.

Consider the matter of fasting. Fasting is probably one of the most under-used spiritual disciplines among believers today. Before the Spirit began speaking, and afterwards, the church fasted. In his book *Celebration of Discipline*, Richard Foster writes, "In a culture where the landscape is dotted with shrines to the golden arches and an assortment of pizza temples, fasting seems out of step with the times."

Someone might say, "Nowhere is fasting commanded in the New Testament, so we're free from such religious rigors of the law." It is correct to say that the New Testament does not command fasting, but it is also correct to say that the New Testament assumes that Christians will fast. Jesus did not say, "If you fast," but rather, "When you fast" (Matthew 6:17). Fasting is assumed to be a practice of those who hunger and thirst after righteousness.

If you are not familiar with that discipline, it refers to abstaining from food for spiritual purposes. The early Christians urged a fast twice a week. Wesley sought to revive the practice among Methodists. Foster's book gives helpful instructions as to the "how" of fasting. The point is, those Christians could see straight. When their stomachs were empty, their minds were focused.

Those early Christians learned of God's will for their church by emptying their lives of distractions and concentrating on Christ. We find the birth of the church's missionary outreach entrenched in prayer and fasting. How do we begin our evangelistic outreach? How do we make major decisions? We have much to learn from the commission of Paul and Barnabas.

THEIR POWER

Knowing something about the commission of Paul and Barnabas, consider the power behind their mission. It is described in verses 4-12.

Do you remember the story? Their first missionary stop was the Island of Cyprus. They visited the city of Paphos. In Paphos they encountered the prophet-magician named Elymas. Elymas exerted great influence in government circles. Verses 6 and 7 show him with the proconsul Sergius Paulus as a resident lobbyist.

When Paul and Barnabas arrived in the city, Sergius Paulus immediately sent for them, hoping to listen to their message. In protest the prophet-magician Elymas tried to turn the proconsul against the Christian faith. Paul must have been furious, because he confronted Elymas to his face. Verse 11 describes how Paul commanded that Elymas become temporarily blind. The proconsul, Sergius Paulus, observed it all; he heard Paul's teaching and he also saw Paul's works.

Verse 12 says that the proconsul believed when he saw what happened. Divine power reinforced their ministry.

Verse 9 describes Paul as being "filled with the Holy Spirit." Paul was empowered and controlled by God and the Holy Spirit. The gospel of Luke says of Jesus in His wilderness temptation that He was "full of the Holy Spirit" (Luke 4:1). That is how Jesus triumphed over Satan. Now in our chapter, Paul confronts the false prophet Elymas, whom he calls a "son of the devil" (v. 10). Hence, just as Jesus was prepared for His confrontation, so was Paul.

Paul sometimes described the Christian life as spiritual warfare. In Ephesians 6 he describes the armor of the Christian. Yet that chapter is preceded by a command for believers to be filled with the Holy Spirit. Preparation for battle includes not only armor but power.

What did the spiritual power of Paul's entail as we examine Acts 13? Three implications can be drawn from these eight verses.

First, by being full of the Holy Spirit, Paul was able to discern spirits. There is no moment of hesitation recorded where Paul tries to ascertain whether Elymas was for him or against him. Paul seems to see right through him. In verse 10 he confronts Elymas by saying, "You who are full of all deceit and fraud, you son of the devil, you enemy of all righteousness, will you not cease to make crooked the straight ways of the Lord?"

In the gospels, John the Baptist is described as a true prophet doing just the opposite. He was not making the things of God sophisticated and difficult. Rather he preached a simple message of repentance. His purpose was to make straight the way of the Lord. Elymas made that way crooked and complicated. He obscured the way of the Lord, and Paul opposed him forthrightly.

Second, by being full of the Holy Spirit, Paul was quick to rely on God's miraculous power. Verse 11 reads, "And now, behold, the hand of the Lord is upon you, and you will be blind and not see the sun for a time."

We do not know what kind of magician Elymas was; he was at least shrewd enough to influence his way into the proconsul's office. Yet it is the power of the Lord that prevailed; the magician was confounded by a greater power.

This missionary journey of Paul and Barnabas cannot be fully understood apart from the part of God. There was something supernatural about their witness. God did great things through them. The power of God changed their lives.

Not long ago I was talking with a woman who had become a Buddhist. I was startled by her Buddhist testimony. After she told me how her practice of chanting had changed her life, I thought to myself, the life of this woman shows more to commend Buddhism than the lives of many Christians show to commend Christ. Something is wrong with evangelism and missionary work if it cannot be explained by the power of God. Paul's life and witness demonstrated the surpassing greatness of the power of God. Whose power does your life demonstrate?

There is also a third observation to be made about the power behind the first missionary journey. By being full of the Spirit, Paul was enabled to teach with power: "Then the proconsul believed when he saw what had happened, being amazed at the teaching of the Lord" (v. 12).

Did you catch that? He believed when he saw, being amazed at the teaching of the Lord. Paul's witness was not just verbal, it was visible. The good deed and the good news were part of the same package. Just as Peter healed the lame man in Jesus' name, so Paul's work made the teaching of the Lord unmistakably clear. And that is how the power of God ought to work in our lives. Being empowered by the Holy Spirit means that what we say and what we do are driven along by our supernatural God to achieve supernatural ends.

THE MESSAGE

Acts 13 tells of one other aspect of this journey. Verses 13-52 record the message of the first missionaries. The message was delivered in Antioch of Pisidia.

As usual, Paul and Barnabas went to the synagogue to worship on the Sabbath. When the time came for the exhortation, Paul received an invitation to speak.

The first part of Paul's sermon reviewed the history of God's grace to Israel. God brought them out of captivity in Egypt. He gave them a land. When they asked for judges, He gave them judges. When they asked for a king, He gave them Saul and David. And from David's offspring, God offered the promise of a Savior.

Then Paul brought his preaching to bear on recent events. John the Baptist proclaimed that the Messiah's coming was at hand. But when Jesus finally did come, Israel rejected Him. In fact, they put Him to death as a criminal.

Now Paul gets very specific. "We preach to you the good news of the promise made to the fathers, that God has fulfilled this promise to our children in that He raised up Jesus" (vv. 32-33).

Here was an Israelite who stood out as categorically different from all others. Moses died. David died and was buried. But Jesus died and rose from the dead.

Did you notice how straightforward Paul's preaching was? He was not holding back, avoiding the name of Jesus for fear of offense.

An elderly minister once received an invitation to pray at his community's high school graduation. An official took him aside and asked that he not refer to the name of Jesus for fear of offending certain members of the community. The pastor responded, "I can never pray, except that I call upon the name of my Savior."

Paul preached Jesus boldly as the fulfillment of God's promise to Israel. And that fact offended some. It was a stumbling block to the Jews and foolishness to the Greeks. And to many it still remains a stumbling stone.

Today, liberal theologians advise against Christian attempts to convert the Jews. But if Paul were alive today, he might leave magicians like Elymas alone. More likely he would occasionally enter a divinity hall and turn the tables. Paul was in a Jewish synagogue, which belonged to dispersed and proselyte Jews in

Asia Minor. And although the great preacher attempted to be all things to all people, he did not water down his message. In the synagogue, he preached Jesus Christ, the Savior of the world. He held fast to one standard of truth, valid for all men in all cultures.

Verses 38-39 take us to the heart of Paul's preaching. He concludes his message by saying, "Therefore let it be known to you, brethren, that through Him forgiveness of sins is proclaimed to you, and through Him everyone who believes is freed from all things, from which you could not be freed through the law of Moses."

So we find two grand concepts here. First, that Jesus offers forgiveness of sins; and second, that in Him we are freed, or literally, justified.

By the forgiveness of sins, Paul offered his audience an opportunity to repent and trust in Christ. All the rebellion of the past could be erased if they looked to Him as the sacrifice for their sins. Guilt and heaviness of heart would be taken away.

And what is more, everyone who believes is justified. God declares us righteous. He has taken our sins and has placed the weight of them on His Son who died for us on the cross. And He has given us His righteousness, so that now God looks on us through His Son. Luther called the taking of our sin and giving of His righteousness "a wonderful exchange."

And it is wonderful. It is worth telling your loved ones about. It is worth sharing with your neighbor, your friends, or your fellow office workers. It is worth passing out tracts and booklets. It is worth sending our sons and daughters as missionaries to the ends of the earth.

That exchange is the gospel of Jesus Christ. It is good news for those who will repent of their sins and believe in Him. But it is bad news for those who ignore Him or shut Him out.

How interesting it is to note the response of those who heard Paul speak. Verse 42 indicates that the Gentiles begged Paul to keep on preaching. Verse 43 tells of the Jewish proselytes who followed Paul and Barnabas and urged them to continue. But verse 50 mentions the Jews who contradicted Paul's message and blasphemed.

The message of a missionary is direct. It concerns ultimate

destiny—eternal life or eternal death! It divides men into two camps: those who follow Jesus Christ, and those who reject Him. And so it is bound to be an offensive message. It is as offensive as Paul and Barnabas. It is as offensive as Jesus. For in the end, a Christian must believe that each man is either a missionary or a mission field. Which are you?

Remember

The two disciples in Antioch trained others and literally worked themselves out of a job.

The Holy Spirit called Paul and Barnabas while the church was in prayer. The Holy Spirit often speaks while we are in prayer.

It is correct to say that the New Testament assumes that Christians will fast.

We must put on the whole armor of God and be filled with the Holy Spirit if we are to succeed.

The good deed and the good news were part of the same package.

The gospel presents two grand concepts: First, that Jesus offers forgiveness of sins; and second, that in Him we are justified.

Questions

1. Describe the state of the Antioch church in Acts 13.
2. When did the Holy Spirit call the missionaries? What was their commission?
3. What does it mean to be empowered by the Holy Spirit?
4. What elements combine to make the missionary's work successful? How do they interrelate? What does it mean to be justified?

Assignment

Consider how the Holy Spirit might be calling you to be a missionary, either in a foreign country or in your own home.

Study how your message is supported by your deeds. Give yourself fully to the control of the Holy Spirit and seek His guidance as you serve as a missionary today.

Acts 14
Church Planting

The mission of the church is missions and the mission of missions is *the church*.

—Unknown

In the year A.D. 532, Emperor Justinian I set out to build a magnificent church in Constantinople called St. Sophia. He summoned the most gifted architects of his day to plan and superintend the project. Ten thousand workmen were employed. Twelve different kinds of marble were brought from around the world, and 320,000 pounds of gold were spent on the enterprise, which practically emptied the emperor's treasury. Gold, silver, ivory, and precious stones were all used for decorative ornamentation. Provincial governors were called on to send their finest relics to the new office.

Justinian pushed his workers relentlessly to finish the project in almost six years. By December 537 the construction was complete. To celebrate the event, the emperor led a solemn procession into the great church. Once inside, Justinian stepped up to the pulpit, raised his hands, and cried, "Glory be to God who has thought me worthy to accomplish so great a' work! O Solomon! I have vanquished you!"

For years, St. Sophia was known as "the great church." Its builder, Justinian, was honored for his monumental achievement.

The apostles of Jesus also built churches. Their construction plans were not quite so elaborate, but the final product was every bit as enduring. Their plans did not call for subsidies from the state treasury, and they did not exhaust ancient mines of precious metals. Their material was mainly flesh and blood. Their architect was the living God. Their foundation was His only Son, Jesus. Their mortar was the Holy Spirit. They built a living monument, one that could grow and spread. Its architecture would not go out of fashion, as did the Byzantine features of St. Sophia. Its construction was not prompted by the will of one man. Its resilience and endurance testify that it could only be an act of God.

The book of Acts says a lot about church building. At first, its focus is the church in Jerusalem. Later, it is the church in Antioch. By chapter 13, Luke directs our attention to the church in Asia Minor. It is evident that the gospel was making its way to the ends of the earth, just as Jesus had commissioned.

Chapter 14 deals with two specific church builders: Paul and Barnabas. But before we examine their methods of construction, it is important to consider the context. To do that we must call to mind the early verses of chapter 13, which describe the leadership in the Antioch church. We find them together worshiping. Acts 13:2 tells us that they were "ministering to the Lord and fasting." They waited on God.

It was at that time, while they were receptive to the voice of God, that the Lord spoke to them. The Holy Spirit said, "Set apart for Me Barnabas and Saul for the work to which I have called them." Verse 4 elaborates on this when it says that they were "sent out by the Holy Spirit."

Any work of church planting must never miss that point. It is the Holy Spirit who calls and sends. We do not appoint ourselves. To do so causes havoc in the church. There are too many self-appointed gurus who work without accountability. Moreover, individuals who appoint themselves also take the liberty to direct themselves. They sometimes become dictators in matters of doctrine. In such a state, they easily slip from apostolic teaching and substitute their own ideas for the gospel.

Also important in chapter 13 is that the church leaders obeyed and confirmed the Spirit's commission. They did not keep Paul and Barnabas for themselves but instead laid their hands on them and sent them out. The church, therefore, ratified the Spirit's calling. They supported the two apostles with prayer and fasting, then they commended them to God's care and sent them out.

That is the background of early church planting. It was a ministry from God. The church merely confirms His call.

But what of the work itself? How did Paul and Barnabas hope to build churches? Is there any discernable procedure to be found in chapter 14? I believe there is. There are at least five steps that probably appeared on most apostolic blueprints. Let us look at them together as they are found in our chapter.

PREACHING

The first activity in planting churches is to preach the gospel. Paul and Barnabas proclaimed that a Savior—the Messiah —had come. They announced deliverance from sin. Men everywhere were called upon to repent and follow Jesus. Their preaching was persistent and forthright. It was not like charades, leaving people to guess what they stood for; it was rather a clear testimony to a Redeemer who had lived, died, and arose again. That Savior commissioned His own messengers to go into all the ancient world to announce the good news.

Paul emphasized the importance of preaching later in his life when he wrote these words in Romans: "How shall they hear without a preacher? . . . How beautiful are the feet of those who bring glad tidings of good things! . . . So faith comes from hearing, and hearing by the word of Christ" (Romans 10:14-17).

Everywhere they went, the message burst forth from their lips. They preached in Salamis, in Paphos, in Pisidian Antioch, in Iconium, in Derbe, and in the cities of Lyconia and Lystra. They preached in towns that were friendly and in towns that were hostile. Regardless of circumstances, they were compulsively addicted to preaching. That is how the Word of God was sown.

Paul and Barnabas preached to a mixed audience. When they entered a city they usually began speaking to people who worshiped the God of Israel. Naturally, their first stop was the Jewish synagogue. One would think that there they would find openness to the gospel of the Messiah. Instead, the Jews were often antagonistic. Many disbelieved and sought to dissuade other Jews and Gentiles who believed. When Paul encountered resistance, he usually left the synagogue and went public with the gospel.

It is interesting to see how Paul approached different groups in his preaching. In 13:16-41 he addresses a predominantly Jewish crowd. Hence, Paul appealed to the common history they shared. His focus was God the Redeemer who fulfilled His promises to David in Jesus of Nazareth. On the other hand, in 14:15-17 we have an excerpt from his message to a strictly Gentile crowd. They worship the gods of the Greek pantheon. Paul exhorts his audience to abandon vain worship and turn to the living God. His starting point is God the Creator. That second speech is interrupted. But assuming Paul would have proceeded as he did with the Gentiles in Athens (chap. 17), we might predict that he would have soon moved on to God's revelation in Christ. So we find that Paul's preaching began with the diverse concerns of his audience but always ended with Jesus Christ.

INTEGRITY

A second step in planting churches is to affirm the gospel with integrity. There is nothing that so discredits the message of the Savior as people who do not appear to be saved. The world sees through inconsistency immediately.

As we saw in chapter 13, the proconsul believes when he sees the Lord's teaching lived out. In 14:3 we see that God "was bearing witness to the word of His grace, granting that signs and wonders be done by their hands." Often in the gospels, miracles are called "signs." They become events that point to something greater. They point to Jesus.

In chapter 13 Elymas loses his sight at Paul's command. In 14:8-10, Paul heals a lame man. Paul's preaching was accompanied by signs of God's power. Those manifested themselves in various ways. But regardless of the manifestation, they affirmed the truth of his message. Sometimes we look upon signs of healing as the supreme apologetic of the church. We ought not. Remember, the people of Lystra missed the point altogether. They thought Paul and Barnabas were gods and began to worship them. The healing of the lame man did not move them to worship Christ. Elsewhere Paul speaks of a greater gift than healing. In 1 Corinthians 13, he explains the more excellent gift of love. Love is a sign as well. In John's gospel, Jesus describes love as the greatest apologetic in the church's arsenal. It is the ultimate proof of Christian integrity. Jesus says in John 13:35, "By this all men will know that you are My disciples, if you have love for one another." In other words, Christlike love in the church is the primary evidence of God's presence in our lives. It authenticates our message. It gives our preaching integrity. That integrity gave Paul's preaching great appeal.

MAKING DISCIPLES

A third step in planting churches is making disciples. It is one thing to claim a convert; it is another to prove one. Verse 21 tells us of Paul and Barnabas at Derbe: "After they preached the gospel to that city and had made many disciples, they returned to Lystra and to Iconium and to Antioch." For those two, preaching and disciple-making went hand-in-hand.

At the time of conversion, a new Christian has a basic knowledge of the Christian faith. He knows that he is a sinner. He knows that Christ died to save sinners. He believes that Christ conquered death and rose again. And he trusts that the merits of Christ's death will save him from eternal separation from God.

Along with that basic knowledge of salvation comes an understanding of baptism, prayer, Scripture, obedience, communion, and the church.

A disciple, however, differs from a convert in that he advances in his understanding and learns to obey all that Jesus commanded (Matthew 28:19-20). A pastor must know how to nurture a convert. Converts need to be established because they are daily assaulted by the world, the flesh, and the devil. Unless we are firmly founded, we will be easily influenced by any sect or false teaching that comes along. That is the vulnerable state that many American Christians find themselves in. According to a recent Gallup report, many people claim to be Christians, but few have a solid biblical and doctrinal foundation. There is a great need for solid Christian teaching and for ethical behavior based on such teaching.

What is it that disciples must learn? Chapter 14 is silent on that. But the answer is simple. Disciples must grow in knowledge and obedience. Or, as the Westminster Shorter Catechism puts it, they must understand "what man is to believe concerning God, and what duty God requires of man." Areas like assurance, temptation, meditation, submission, worship, God's moral law, and Christian doctrine must become familiar to them. They must be taught to think Christianly, to think along the Bible in order to integrate their confession with their profession.

A problem with some churches is that they are filled with infant Christians who have yet to be established. They are not taught to stand on their own two feet and penetrate the world in Christ's name. Instead, they fear the world and are vulnerable to its every assault.

The apostles were out to make disciples, not parasites. Paul aimed to make Christians mature in Christ (Ephesians 4:13). James spoke of Christians becoming "complete, lacking in nothing" (James 1:4). How does your church measure up?

Discipleship is all about taking the faith seriously. The world does not like this, of course. It makes obedience a costly endeavor. You will remember that at nearly every stop in their journey, Paul and Barnabas were opposed. Verse 4 reads, "but the multitude . . . was divided." The disbelieving Jews, says verse 2, "stirred up the minds of the Gentiles, and embittered them against the brethren." The *New King James Version* says that they "poisoned their minds." This opposition was aimed at both the apostles and their converts.

Amidst such opposition, the young Christians needed help. If they were abandoned, they would have had much difficulty remaining steadfast. They needed direction from their spiritual parents.

It would have been easy for Paul and Barnabas to walk away from those life-threatening situations. After being stoned and dragged out of towns we would expect to find them packing their bags and heading back to Antioch. But verse 21 startles us with these words: "They returned to Lystra and to Iconium and to Antioch [of Pisidia]." They returned to the places where the persecution had been most intense.

The apostles knew that disciple-making *takes time.* Disciples and disciple-makers need to be together. Disciples need to see the integrity of faith in the lives of their shepherds. There is nothing so persuasive and instructive as a godly example. In an age when ministry has degenerated to professionalism and church-building to technique, we need to see again the power of diligent flesh-to-flesh discipleship. That essential activity rarely takes place over the airwaves. It is only in a person-to-person contact that true discipleship takes place. It is a job of the church that can never be preempted by the media.

APPOINTING ELDERS

That brings us to a fourth step in church planting mentioned in our chapter. Paul and Barnabas appointed elders. What is left unmentioned, however, is that they also trained men for that work. In Ephesians 3 Paul says that it is the job of the pastor-teacher to train others for the work of the ministry. So Paul and Barnabas built up leaders from among the larger group of disciples.

Now remember, this was a missionary journey of limited duration. Yet notice the time that the apostles took in one region. They stayed until the church was established. The exact length of time in each city is uncertain. But it was surely not a hit-and-run operation. They stayed long enough to develop indigenous leadership. Verse 23 tells us that after returning to those cities, "they appointed elders for them in every church."

An elder is an overseer. Paul followed a pattern of leadership as practiced in the synagogues. Certain men were charged to instruct, administer, and discipline the Christian assembly. At that point in time, the term *elder* may not have been an official church office. Church organization was still somewhat fluid, and various terms were used. Later, Paul calls them "overseers" and compares them to shepherds (20:28). What is important is that Paul and Barnabas appointed leaders to take their place when they were gone. Although it may seem that Paul violates the admonition of 1 Timothy 3 about not making overseers out of new converts, we should remember that he was aided by the Spirit's direction in the first church planting mission. Rightly, the leadership was appointed after carefully seeking out God's will. As is characteristic of apostolic decision-making, prayer with fasting is the usual means of learning the mind of God. Decision-making was not primarily democratic, or oligarchic, or even dictatorial. It was a theocratic enterprise in which all of God's people came to a consensus on what God desired.

COMMENDING AND REPORTING

After turning the leadership over to the elders, Paul and Barnabas were ready to return to Antioch. In their leaving we learn one final aspect of church planting. The apostles commended those new churches to the Lord, and then reported to the home church in Antioch all that had taken place.

Verse 23 reads, "They commended them to the Lord in whom they had believed." The apostles trained their people to depend, not on their own fleeting presence, but on God's abiding presence. The apostles had to let go of their spiritual children and commit their progress in the gospel to the Lord.

Verse 26 says that Paul and Barnabas then sailed to Antioch, "from which they had been commended to the grace of God for the work that they had accomplished." Obviously, commendation to God's grace was a common practice. Like Paul and Barnabas, the Antioch church was not paralyzed with worry over the results of the first missionary journey. It trusted God to care for the details. God was faithful and the job was accomplished. In the same way, Paul and Barnabas now looked to God to complete the work among the new disciples in Asia Minor.

Verse 27 brings us back to where we started. Paul and Barnabas were sent out by a particular church—not as free agents. So it is natural that they should report to the mother church about their progress. The results of their journey had a revolutionary effect on the Christian faith. In Paul's words, God "had opened a door of faith to the Gentiles" (v. 27).

The news sent tremors throughout the ancient Christian world. They were felt especially in Jerusalem.

To many, Paul's Gentile outreach signaled a betrayal of Judaism. Paul encouraged Gentiles to come to God apart from the customs of Moses. Is it any wonder that chapter 14 ends, "And they spent a long time with the disciples [in Antioch]"? Paul had a lot of explaining to do; the Jewish Christians had a lot of questions. There was controversy and conflict that would prompt a major confrontation in Jerusalem (chap. 15).

It is crucial that we understand the nature of this mission. The priority of Paul and Barnabas's faith was not external but an internal personal relationship to God in Christ. The structure that they built was an organic building. It was a household of faith (Ephesians 3:19). It was a holy Temple (Ephesians 3:21). It was a monument of the life of God that came upon men in Jesus Christ. It is a monument that can be seen today. Not primarily in the great cathedrals of the West but in the community of the worldwide Body of those who claim Christ as Lord and Savior.

D. L. Moody once said that he had no interest in being remembered by monuments of stone. They will crumble. The only monument he wanted was the lives of men and women who would carry the gospel to the ends of the earth. That is why he founded the Moody Bible Institute.

Moody's concerns are a distant echo of Jesus' thoughts on church building. The great Temple, Jesus predicted, would be destroyed. But the temple of His body would endure forever.

You are a part of that Body. You stand as His monument. I commend you to God's grace and pray that He will accomplish His acts through you.

Remember

"Faith comes from hearing, and hearing by the word of Christ" (Romans 10:17).

There is nothing that discredits the message of the Savior like people who do not appear to be saved.

For Paul and Barnabas, preaching and disciple-making went hand-in-hand.

Christians must be taught to think Christianly, to think along with the Bible in order to integrate their confession with their profession.

The priority of Paul and Barnabas's faith was not external but an internal personal relationship with God in Christ.

Questions

1. How might contemporary preaching or witnessing begin with the concerns of modern man and lead to the good news of Jesus?
2. How is God's power manifest in your church? What about your own life?
3. What category do you fall into: Are you a new convert, a disciple, or a leader in the church? What are the qualifications of each of those positions? What steps are the most important in discipleship?
4. What is an elder according to 1 Timothy?
5. How did God open a door of faith to the Gentiles, and what consequences did that have in the early church?

Assignment

Name as many metaphors as you can for the church. See Ephesians 2:11-22 and 1 Corinthians 12. How then must we define the church? What must we aim at in starting new churches? Should a building with a steeple be called a church?

Acts 15
The Council of Jerusalem

[Prejudice is] the mistreatment of people without their having done anything to merit such mistreatment. It has been a source of human unhappiness and misunderstanding wherever and whenever it has arisen.

— Arnold Rose

Each star differs in size and shape. So does each leaf. Flowers differ in color and fragrance; people differ in attitude and approach; no two fingerprints are the same. In life, difference abounds. The challenge is what we do with our differences, and what our distinctions do to us.

The early church experienced a spontaneous expansion. It was inevitable that differences among Christians would arise. One of the major areas of contention involved the presence of Gentile believers in a Jewish-dominated church. Acts 15 deals with the clash between those two groups and how they resolved their differences at the Council of Jerusalem in A.D. 49.

The Dissension in the Jerusalem Church

For the first few decades the infant apostolic church had no part of the written New Testament books to guide them. To most Jewish believers, Christianity brought to completion their Judaism. They found it difficult to believe that anyone could really be acceptable to God apart from the ancient Jewish order.

Cornelius the Gentile and his family were exceptions. However, as large numbers of Gentiles responded to the gospel, some Jews began to teach that circumcision and the keeping of the Mosaic law were necessary for salvation. Opposition to non-Jewish Christianity was formulated and intensified.

On the other hand, the new Gentile converts viewed Jesus of Nazareth as the Savior of the whole world. They understood Jesus' background as a Jew and that He came from the seed of Abraham. They were grateful for that but saw no reason to submit to Jewish rituals and the Mosaic law.

Paul and Barnabas immediately understood that those "in house" differences were not minor but major. It was not merely a uniqueness of culture or fellowship but the difference between salvation by God's grace and salvation by man's works. If left uncared for, it would split the believers along racial lines, and any progress the gospel had made would be destroyed.

Paul and Barnabas went to visit the Jerusalem church. "And when they arrived at Jerusalem, they were received by the church . . . and they reported all that God had done with them. But certain ones of the sect of the Pharisees who had believed, stood up, saying, 'It is necessary to circumcise them, and to direct them to observe the Law of Moses' " (vv. 4-5).

Many things in life are not worth great struggle, but Paul and Barnabas saw this difference as fundamental. Someone has said that "if you don't stand for something, you'll fall for anything." Though Paul and Barnabas may have had disagreements with their fellow believers on some minor issues, the time had come to take a firm position. The dissension in the Jerusalem church became a major matter. Any addition to salvation by God's grace alone is a major cause for dissension. It must be faced and settled in every decade.

THE DISCUSSION OF THE JERUSALEM COUNCIL

The leaders of the church gathered together in consultation with the two representatives from Antioch. Peter began the council session by reminding them of God's acceptance of the Gentiles. Notice verses 7-8: "And after there had been much debate, Peter stood up, and said to them, 'Brethren, you know that in the early days God made a choice among you, that by my mouth the Gentiles should hear the word of the gospel and believe. And God, who knows the heart, bore witness to them, giving them the Holy Spirit, just as He also did to us.' "

Peter announced that a good while ago God had already made it clear that the Gentiles should hear and believe the gospel. Peter said, "This was God's decision and not ours." Also, the Gentiles received the Holy Spirit, a positive sign of sonship and acceptance by God.

Then Peter concluded by affirming that through the grace of Jesus Christ, Jew and Gentile alike can be saved. "Respect of persons" is inconsistent with God's love and grace.

After Peter addressed the council, Paul and Barnabas spoke. They agreed with Peter as they shared the miracles and wonders of God among the Gentiles from their missionary travels: "And all the multitude kept silent, and they were listening to Barnabas and Paul as they were relating what signs and wonders God had done through them among the Gentiles" (v. 12).

Finally it came time for James, the leader of the Jerusalem church, to wrap up the discussion. He did so by quoting the Scriptures. For James, the Word of God took prominence. Experience has its place and can teach us many important lessons, but what God says stands supreme.

Henry Ward Beecher said, "The Bible is God's chart for you to steer by, to keep you from the bottom of the sea, and to show you where the harbor is, and how to reach it without running on rocks or bars." In any area of our life we need to understand that the will of God and the Word of God are inseparable. The Bible is our ultimate authority.

However, a danger also exists in going too far in the other direction. A cartoon character was found surrounded by his Bible and various reference books. When asked what he was doing the character responded, "I'm looking for some Bible verses to back up my preconceived ideas." Let us not take the approach that says, "Here's what I believe, now how can I support it from Scripture?" The Jerusalem Council based their conclusions on the Word of God and formulated their doctrines from that point.

Notice verses 15-18: "And with this the words of the Prophets agree, just as it is written, 'After these things I will return, and

I will rebuild the tabernacle of David which has fallen . . . in order that the rest of mankind may seek the Lord . . . who makes these things known from of old.' "

James tells us that God has not abandoned the kingdom for Israel; but in the meantime, He is calling out from the Gentiles a people for His name.

THE DECISION OF THE JERUSALEM COUNCIL

Verse 19 reads, "Therefore it is my judgment that we do not trouble those who are turning to God from among the Gentiles." How was the decision reached? Not in the democratic process we are so accustomed to—it was not moved and then seconded and carried by a majority.

A danger exists in assuming that the majority is right. The majority, when against the Word of God, results in tragedy. Remember the people of Israel responding to the twelve spies. By far the vast majority sided with the ten spies. Only two from the entire nation sided with God. And only those two entered the land and received the blessings.

Verse 28 reads, "For it seemed good to the Holy Spirit and to us to lay upon you no greater burden than these essentials."

The Jerusalem church earnestly wanted the mind of the Lord, and when that became clear, it announced its decision to the Christians in Antioch, Syria, and Cilicia. The council affirmed the principle of salvation *by grace alone*. The Mosaic law was not needed for salvation.

This decision resulted in victory for free grace—not cheap grace. Gentile believers were free from the yoke of the law. However, their liberty was not to result in license. James continues, "That you abstain from things sacrificed to idols and from blood and from things strangled and from fornication; if you keep yourselves free from such things, you will do well" (v. 29).

The church accepted the decision of James. That averted a disastrous split. It settled a doctrinal matter once and for all. Though the problem arose again and again, the issue was settled by the Jerusalem Council.

Three major results came from the Jerusalem Council's decision:

First, because of the decisions of Acts 15 we can freely say and sing,

> Free from the law, O happy condition,
> Jesus hath bled, and there is remission;
> Cursed by the law and bruised by the fall,
> Grace hath redeemed us once for all.
>
> (Philip P. Bliss)

Second, because of the decision of Acts 15 we can enthusiastically affirm that salvation is by God's grace alone, apart from works of any kind. Ordinances have their place for sure but never for salvation. To condition salvation upon any ritual, rite, or ceremony takes salvation out of the realm of grace and places it in the realm of works.

And third, the emancipated life does not mean the unrestrained life. We are called to godliness and holiness. We are to keep ourselves unspotted in an evil world. Grace means giving no offense—neither to the Jew, nor the Gentile, nor to the church of God (1 Corinthians 10:32).

The decision of Acts 15 announces that a Jew or Gentile through faith in Jesus Christ alone can know the forgiveness of sins. Religion says, "Something in my hands I bring," but gospel salvation says, "Nothing in my hands I bring; simply to Thy cross I cling."

How do we solve our differences? Peter shared what God was doing in the conversion of Cornelius and his family. Paul and Barnabas did the same. They explained that Gentiles believed in Jesus Christ. Then James applied the Word of God.

May we too be sensitive to what God is doing and test it by the Word of God. That is what God wants us to do with all our differences.

Remember

Any addition to salvation by God's grace alone is a major cause for dissension and must be faced and settled in every decade.

Experience has its place and can teach us many important lessons, but what God says stands supreme.

The church earnestly wanted the mind of the Lord, and when that was clear, it became the mind of the church.

Religion says, "Something in my hands I bring," but gospel salvations says, "Nothing in my hands I bring; simply to Thy cross I cling."

Questions

1. Describe the positions on both sides of the debate at the Jerusalem Council. Give reasons behind each position.
2. What impact did the Word of God have upon the final decision of the council?
3. After the decision, the council requested two types of behavior from the Gentile Christians. What were they? Why do you think the council requested that behavior?
4. What effects did the results of the council's decision have upon the Gentile Christians? Upon Christians today?

Assignment

Analyze how you deal with differences of opinion when they come up. How can you bring your resolution process into line with that used by the Jerusalem Council? Determine to seek God's guidance for your decisions in the future.

Acts 16
A Miracle at Midnight

The refusal to choose is a form of choice; disbelief is a form of belief.

— Frank Barron

Small opportunities are often the beginning of great enterprises.

— Demosthenes

Moments of disaster often mark the beginning of a brand-new day. It might be the catastrophe of suffering, as in the case of Job. It could be the tragedy of failure, as in the denials of Peter, or the destructive forces of nature, like the storm on the Sea of Galilee, which threatened to sink the disciples' boat.

Sometimes calamity comes because we have drifted away from the Lord. But severe difficulties also come to those who are living as they should. Both such occasions are found in Acts 16.

God had called Paul and Silas to go into distant Europe and preach the good news to the Gentiles. Yet in spite of that call, they found themselves unjustly thrown in jail. Their catastrophe was one of injustice.

Having settled into dungeon conditions, Acts 16:25 reports that "about midnight Paul and Silas were praying and singing hymns of praise to God, and the prisoners were listening to them." Paul and Silas were in a Roman jail, probably surrounded by the shady, shabby criminal element of Philippi. Then at midnight, when even a prisoner likes to get his sleep, Paul and Silas began to pray and sing.

It is always appropriate to pray. Perhaps Paul and Silas did not know what else to do. Their plans for carrying out God's will seemed disrupted. Their itinerary did not include a stop at the Philippian jail; but in response to catastrophe they turned to God.

Along with praying, they also sang praise to God. That was probably Europe's first sacred concert—a musical so overwhelming that it literally brought the house down. Verse 26 reads, "And suddenly there came a great earthquake." The jail house shook, the earth's foundation broke up, the prison walls cracked, the doors flung open, and the chains fell off. Paul and Silas were free.

Consider the three consequences of the catastrophe in Acts 16: The jailer's question, the disciples' answer, and the jailer's response.

THE JAILER'S QUESTION

Verse 30 records the jailer's immediate response to the earthquake, "Sirs, what must I do to be saved?" Why did he ask that of Paul and Silas? He probably sneered when he first heard them causing a late-night commotion in his dungeon. Having traced those loud melodies and prayers to the source, he observed at firsthand the unusual worship of Paul and Silas. When the walls shook, the jailer must have immediately connected the earthquake to their prayers, for he cried directly to the two disciples with his desperate plea for salvation.

His question was a personal question. He asked, "What must I do to be saved?" Think about who he addressed his question to. Standing right before him was the brilliant apostle Paul. Paul was a theologian whose great theme was the grace of God. He wrote that salvation is the gift of God. He said that we do not earn our salvation by a works righteousness; rather, we receive it. We are saved by grace through faith (Ephesians 2:8-9). That is the teaching that made Paul famous.

Yet notice what Paul does. He does not get theologically sophisticated and break into a discourse on God's unconditional election. Neither does he rhapsodize on predestination as he does in Ephesians 1. Instead, he takes the jailer's question at face value. The jailer wanted to know what *he* as an individual should do to be saved. So Paul told a repentant man what he needed to do.

God calls, but I must answer. God knocks at the door of my life, and I must open it. Salvation is a marvelous work of God, but we must respond to God's tug. The question of Acts 16 is a personal question calling for a personal response.

Some time ago, I spoke to a man and asked him if he were a Christian. "No," he said, "I'm waiting for God to do something."

I said, "Friend, God loves you. Christ came to this world and went to the cross to die for sinners. When the Lord Jesus left the earth, the Holy Spirit came to convict sinners and to call them to repentance. God has done all that He is going to do. If you're ever to know God's salvation, you must respond to what God has provided."

You may be just a number at work or one small face in a sea of mankind, but in the sight of God, you are loved. How will you answer His call?

The jailer's question was prompted by a catastrophe. A great earthquake had occurred. The jailhouse had collapsed. The jailer feared that his prisoners had escaped. If they had, according to Roman law, his life was in danger.

I have lived long enough to discover that moments of catastrophe often signal the beginning of a brand-new start, an opportunity to begin all over again. It was that way for the Philippian jailer of Acts 16.

Some time ago a veteran in a wheelchair approached me. He told how he had been severely wounded in Vietnam. As I expressed my sympathy he said, "You don't have to be sorry. I'm glad God permitted me to suffer, because it was in my difficult hour that a fellow soldier related the claims of Christ to me. I heard the knocking of God through my pain, and I opened my life to Jesus Christ."

THE DISCIPLES' ANSWER

What answer did Paul give to the jailer's question? He provided a thrilling answer. You do not have to have a seminary degree to understand it. Paul simply turned to the man and said, "Believe in the Lord Jesus, and you shall be saved, you and your household" (v. 31).

Paul's answer was not, "Let's wait until the excitement is over." No, Paul had no fear of a little excitement. There is no doubt that we live in an age of misplaced emotion. We can get excited about a ball game or a new car; we can shed tears over a meaningless television program. But do we get excited about the things of God? Can we get excited about people's souls?

Paul was not afraid of authentic excitement. When he preached, usually people were either glad or mad, there was either a revival or a riot—but rarely did they remain neutral.

Sometime ago I heard of a country preacher who said, "I don't really mind how high they jump or how loud they shout so long as when they hit the ground they walk straight." Salvation is an exciting thing. The souls of people are worth getting excited about.

Paul did not say, "Let's wait until morning." Nor did he say, "Let's wait until everything is returned to the status quo." His response was not, "When everything is normal, then we'll discuss the implications of salvation." No, simply and in a straightforward manner he gave a pointed answer: "Believe in the Lord Jesus, and you shall be saved."

As he answered the question there was no indication that the jailer would have to change his environment. Sometimes it may be necessary to change your employment or other circumstances, but Paul did not deal with the jailer's environment. Paul dealt with the issue at hand, and that was the attitude of the jailer's soul toward Jesus Christ.

Conversion occurs in two major steps: The first is repentance. You may say, "Paul never told this man to repent." No, there was no reason to. His repentance was obvious. Prior to the earthquake, the jailer had Paul and Silas bound and beaten, put in stocks and chains, and placed in an inner cell. Prior to the earthquake, they were villains, rabble-rousers, criminals.

But after the earthquake, he knelt at their feet. After the earthquake, he trembled (v. 29). After the earthquake he said, "Sirs, what must I do to be saved?" The man's repentance was so plain that Paul, seeing that repentant, broken, trembling man, simply said, "Believe in the Lord Jesus, and you shall be saved."

No one will ever see heaven apart from repentance. Unless a man repents and turns from sin and self, he will never know the peace and forgiveness of God.

A certain pastor was trying to communicate the concept of repentance to his congregation. After he had struggled for a time, a deacon stood and walked toward the front of the church. As he walked down the aisle, he said, "I'm going to hell, I'm going to hell, I'm going to hell." Then, turning around in front of the congregation and walking back up the aisle, he said, "But now I'm going to heaven, I'm going to heaven." As he sat down, he said, "That is repentance."

What is repentance? It is a change of direction. It is a change of mind. It is a change of heart and attitude; and it results in a change of conduct.

The second step in conversion is faith. "For by grace you have been saved through faith; and that not of yourselves, it is the gift of God" (Ephesians 2:8-9).

What is it to believe in Christ? It is to trust Him, to cast your life upon Him for forgiveness, for His will and control.

THE JAILER'S RESPONSE

Verses 33-34 tell the response of the jailer.

First, it was an immediate response: "He took them that very hour of the night." The hour was late; it was midnight. It was a difficult hour. An earthquake had devastated the place. It was inconvenient to believe in that hour. Nevertheless, his response was swift, immediate.

Second, it was a total response. The jailer washed their wounds (v. 33). He brought them into his own house and set food before them (v. 34). What a wonderful change it was in his life. And he was baptized immediately, along with his family (v. 33).

The gospel call that Paul and Silas gave the jailer goes out to you today. "Believe in the Lord Jesus, and you shall be saved."

Remember

Prayer is always appropriate.

God calls, but I must answer. God knocks at the door of my life, but I must open it.

Catastrophe often signals the beginning of a brand-new start, an opportunity to begin all over again.

Salvation is an exciting thing. The souls of people are worth getting excited about.

No one will ever see God's heaven apart from repentance.

Repentance is a change of direction. It is a change of mind, heart, and attitude; and it results in a change of conduct.

Questions

1. What relationship existed between the two missionaries and God at the time they were arrested and thrown in jail? How did their relationship affect the incident?
2. What significance is there in the fact that the jailer's question was personal?
3. How is it that catastrophe often signals a new start?
4. What is meant by the sentence, "We live in an age of misplaced emotion"?
5. What are the two major steps in conversion, and why are they important?
6. Describe the response of the jailer when his question was answered.

Assignment

Think about the catastrophes that have affected your life. Analyze how they changed your life. If that change took the wrong direction, repent of that direction, and turn to follow God's leadings.

Acts 17
Three Responses to the Resurrection

Defer no time, delays have dangerous ends.
— William Shakespeare

How should a child of God conduct himself in a non-Christian environment? Acts 17 pictures the apostle Paul waiting for his friends in the famous city of Athens, the intellectual capital of the ancient world.

Verse 16 reads, "Now while Paul was waiting for them at Athens, his spirit was being provoked in him as he was beholding the city full of idols." Man-made deities appeared to be everywhere.

Some have criticized Paul for being artistically insensitive. On the contrary, Paul enjoyed the beautiful, but he opposed idolatry. There is nothing wrong with enjoying beautiful things; in fact, balance and beauty find their sources in God and His creation. But Paul was deeply disturbed by the idolatry and the false religion represented in Athens. Those images signified not the artistic talents of the Athenians but their misdirected worship.

The Scripture says Paul was "provoked." The hundreds of images threw him into inner turmoil. He felt sorrow and anger at the same time. Men and women were created to worship the true God, but they had "exchanged the glory of the incorruptible God for an image in the form of corruptible man and of birds and four-footed animals and crawling creatures" (Romans 1:23).

Verse 17 pictures Paul disputing with them in the synagogues and the marketplace on a daily basis. Then some Epicurean and Stoic philosophers brought him before their council to hear more of Paul's message.

Paul began by saying that there are many gods but only one true God, the God who made the world. That Creator God will one day judge the world. The inescapable proof of a coming judgment is the resurrection of Jesus from the dead.

When they heard of the resurrection of the dead, three attitudes were expressed (v. 32): some mocked, some delayed, and some believed.

SOME MOCKED

The first attitude involved mockery by some of the men. As a young man, I became upset by those who mocked God. Then I began to realize that those people used mockery as their response to the gospel.

In Genesis 6, some mocked Noah when he predicted a judgment by water. But in spite of the mockers, judgment came. When Abraham and Lot predicted judgment for Sodom and Gomorrah, some mocked. But judgment came. When Lot warned his family in Genesis 19:14, the Scripture says, "He appeared to his sons-in-law to be jesting." But judgment came. Throughout history a percentage has always mocked when hearing the message of God.

Matthew 27:28-29 describes the crucifixion of Jesus: "And they stripped Him, and put a scarlet robe on Him. And after weaving a crown of thorns, they put it on His head, and a reed in His right hand; and they kneeled down before Him and mocked Him, saying, 'Hail, King of the Jews!' "

Instead of sitting on a throne fit for a king, He hung on a cross. Instead of wearing a golden diadem, they gave Him a crown of thorns. Instead of a kingdom, they placed Him in the shrunken, narrow dimensions of a borrowed tomb. They mocked Him.

Paul the apostle was writing to the Galatians when he said, "Do not be deceived, God is not mocked; for whatever a man sows, this he will also reap." Remember that you reap exactly what you sow. No more, no less. You cannot mock God and get away with it.

Genesis 39 tells how the sons of Jacob were envious of Joseph and how they tried to mock their father, Jacob. Joseph was kidnapped and sold as a slave. Then the brothers brought his coat stained with blood back to their father. Their father imagined the details: "Some wild beast has devoured Joseph." They mocked their father.

Ultimately, Joseph rose to a position of leadership. He assumed the office of second in command in the land of Egypt. Famine came to the land, and Genesis 45:3 pictures Joseph's brothers before him in order to buy food to keep them alive through the famine. They were terrified at Joseph's presence. Why? Because their sin had found them out.

Today some people mock the resurrection of Jesus by denying it ever occurred. Various alternatives are set forth to explain the resurrection story.

Some say that the doctrine of the resurrection is a deliberate invention of the church. But that is not valid in light of the great number of eyewitnesses. In A.D. 56 Paul tells us that more than five hundred original witnesses to the resurrection were still alive. Those who doubted at that time had ample opportunity to prove the resurrection false. All they were able to formulate were theories that failed to meet the facts.

Then too, the early Scriptures went out to the known world with the collective authority of the whole church, not the backing of only two or three imposters.

Consider also the character of the witnesses. They were people of integrity, living above reproach.

Others mock by saying that Jesus never literally arose. Like Thomas they say, "Unless I shall see in His hands the imprint of the nails, and put my finger into the place of the nails, and put my hand into His side, I will not believe" (John 20:25).

Later Jesus said to Thomas, "Reach here your finger, and see My hands; and reach here your hand, and put it into My side;

and be not unbelieving, but believing" (John 20:27). Thomas was convinced against his will.

Still others say that the disciples stole the body of Jesus. In other words, Matthew, Mark, Luke, John, Peter, and Paul are all liars. But those men taught that it was wrong to lie. Can you believe that they would invent and circulate a lie? And what did they do with the body of Jesus if they had taken it?

Remember also that people will not die for what they know to be a lie. All the apostles, save one, died a martyr's death for their belief that Jesus Christ rose from the dead.

Some said the disciples did not steal the body, but the local authorities did. If that were the case, why did they not produce the body when the followers of Jesus began to fill Jerusalem and all of the civilized world with the message of resurrection?

Finally, the writer of *The Passover Plot* suggested that Jesus never really died but that He fell into an unconscious condition —not really dead, but apparently dead. That theory supposes that as a result of the crucifixion Jesus swooned. Then, because the tomb was cool, He revived. But how could He roll away the stone in that condition? And why did the soldiers fail to stop Him? And how could He walk on wounded feet? And where did He go from there? Even skeptics agree that the "swooning" solution is absurd.

Some Delayed

Another response to the gospel is that some delayed. Verse 32 reads, "We shall hear you again concerning this." Was this just stalling to get rid of Paul? They seemed to say, "Not now, but later." Most people are not so much against God as they are preoccupied.

In Jesus' parable of the five wise and five foolish virgins we are told, "And while they were going away to make the purchase, the bridegroom came, and those who were ready went in with him to the wedding feast; and the door was shut" (Matthew 25:10). The foolish virgins were not God-haters; they were not anti-bridegroom. Theirs was the sin of neglect and delay. They had no oil because they were preoccupied.

The book of Numbers tells of the children of Israel at the border town of Kadesh Barnea. There they acted in unbelief. They missed their chance. The Lord said, "The land is yours. It is my gift to you." But they failed to possess it.

Into every life there comes a Kadesh Barnea. We are what we are because of what we do with our opportunities. At Kadesh Barnea they said they would not follow God, they would not move out in faith, they would not believe; and for forty years they wandered through the wilderness until all except Caleb and Joshua died. It was the longest funeral march in history.

SOME BELIEVED

Some mocked, others delayed. But verse 34 tells us that "some men joined him and believed."

Paul dealt with a tough crowd—the philosophers of Athens. Originally, Paul encountered Epicureans and Stoics. But by the time he reached the Areopagus, other philosophical schools must have been represented as well.

Two extremes were predominant in Greek philosophy. There were the transcendentalists, who said that God was absolutely separate from the concerns of earth because matter itself was evil. And there were the immanentists, who held to a form of pantheism, identifying God with the world.

The reason why Paul was such an oddity in that Greek forum can in part be explained by the middle-of-the-road doctrine of God the Redeemer. According to Paul, God was not so otherworldly that He could not come in contact with the earth, and He was not so identified with it that the world had no need of a Savior.

Paul claimed that God was Lord of heaven and earth. He made all things. He involved Himself in history. He sent His Son to redeem mankind. The Son died and then conquered death by rising again; and He will come again to judge the world.

To Greek ears, that was a new message indeed. How shocked then some of the council must have been when some of their own, like Dionysius, took a public stand for Christ.

Paul's doctrine of God was mind-boggling. He spoke of a

holy God who was also loving—of a Creator who was also a Redeemer.

After introducing his audience to the claims of Christ, Paul moved with boldness to ask for a response. He wanted to know what those sophisticated Greeks would do with Jesus. Some were eager to believe. Some were probably as anxious as the Philippian jailer, asking, "What must I do to be saved?"

Paul's answer was simple. He told them that God was "declaring to men that all everywhere should repent" (v. 30).

The ones who believed moved beyond a vague belief in God. They entered a personal relationship with Him in Christ. That was a startling moment for Greek minds. It was a recognition that the aggressive, creative love of God was more real than all the magnificent statues of the Greek pantheon combined.

Have you found that love and power to be real in your life? Have you believed on Him?

Some Greeks preferred to worship their dumb idols rather than acknowledge Jesus Christ as God's provision for sin. Others remained undecided. But in their case, not to decide was a decision against Christ. Yet some of them believed and had their lives invaded by the mighty power of God.

Remember

There is nothing wrong with enjoying beautiful things; in fact, balance and beauty find their sources in God and His creation.

Mockery is one response to the gospel. Throughout history a percentage has always mocked when hearing the message of God.

You reap exactly what you sow: no more, no less. You cannot mock God and get away with it.

We are what we are because of what we do with our opportunities.

Not to decide is to decide against Christ.

Questions

1. In what ways do people mock Jesus' resurrection today?
2. List the four major theories that deny the resurrection. How would you counter each of those theories?
3. How is it that delay is a means of mocking God?
4. Why was Paul such an oddity to the Greek philosophers?

Assignment

Check your church library for books that present evidences for Christianity, and make a list of those evidences that demonstrate that Jesus rose from the dead.

Acts 18
Passing the Torch

He that gives good advice builds with one hand; he that gives good counsel and example builds with both; but he that gives good admonition and bad example builds with one hand and pulls down with the other.
— Francis Bacon

I was deeply stirred as I watched the passing of the Olympic torch on its way to the 1984 Olympic games in Los Angeles. The torch began its travels in the valley of Olympia in Greece. Weeks before the games, runners carried it in a cross-country relay over thousands of miles. When it reached our American shores, the torch was passed on by ordinary people through our towns, cities, and farmlands. I recall one scene where rural people, before dawn, came out to the road in their bathrobes. As the runner drew near, some flashed a thumbs up sign. Then a soft, startling cheer broke the silence.

That torch traversed many countries and states. It passed through the hands of countless runners before it reached Los Angeles.

Do you remember the final runner who carried it into the Olympic stadium? The crowd cheered as the torch went once around the track, then up the stairs where it finally lit the giant Olympic flame.

The Olympic torch is a symbol of international brotherhood, and the relay is a reminder to pass that spirit on. The president of the Olympic committee called the torch "a symbol that the Olympic ideal still lives."

We believe in passing on important things. Each day we make our children wait for a bus that takes them to school where they will be trained. There they learn skills, values, and traditions important to our history.

The church believes in passing on important things as well. Perhaps you send your children to a Christian school. You want them to learn Christian principles. Whereas children in the state schools sing songs about Washington, and children in Marxist countries sing songs about Lenin, the children in Christian schools sing about Jesus.

Jesus also passed on important things. He never wrote a book. Instead, He invested His life in twelve men. Before He departed, He commissioned them, saying, "Go therefore and make disciples of all the nations, baptizing them in the name of the Father and the Son and the Holy Spirit, teaching them to observe all that I commanded you" (Matthew 28:19-20).

Jesus passed on important things by making disciples, and Paul adopted Jesus' methods. In 2 Timothy 2:2 Paul writes to one of his own disciples saying, "The things which you have heard from me in the presence of many witnesses, these entrust to faithful men, who will be able to teach others also."

What Paul describes there is well illustrated in Acts 18. There we see Christian disciple-making in action. Paul left Athens for Corinth in order to pass the light of Christ on to others. Like an Olympic torchbearer, he handed the gospel flame to other runners. Such disciple-making became the secret weapon of the church.

Look for a moment at three Olympic-like runners in Acts 18. Watch the flaming torch as it passed from hand to hand.

THE FIRST RUNNER

The first runner in our study is Paul. Fresh from the intellectual center of Athens, Paul now faced the challenge of a famed commercial city. Corinth was a seaport on the main trade route from the Orient to Rome. It was the place where East and West met. As a result, it was also a city with many temples to many different deities. By far the most famous was the temple of Venus, the goddess of love. That was not the sterile white temple that we see in our twentieth-century replicas. The temple priests owned more than a thousand prostitutes. They rented them out day-by-day to tourists and sailors, just as some of the major hotels in Hong Kong and Bangkok hire out prostitutes today.

When Paul settled in Corinth he began working as a tent-maker. It was the custom of rabbis in those days to be self-supporting. Paul linked up with two other tentmakers named Aquila and Priscilla, who were refugees from Rome. When not working at his trade, Paul could be found at the synagogue preaching.

There are two activities that are crucial for disciples. We see them both exemplified in Paul.

First, Paul was constantly contending for the faith. He was always seeking to persuade. Verse 4 says that he argued in the synagogue every Sabbath and persuaded Jews and Greeks. In Athens we saw how he argued with the Greeks. Now here he is with the Corinthian Jews. In Athens he argued that "Jesus is the risen one." Now in the synagogue he argues that "Jesus is the promised one." In either case, his message centered on Jesus Christ as God's agent of salvation.

Paul was not always successful. In verse 6 we see that he was strongly opposed. There was no evangelistic crusade in Corinth, no churches to cooperate. Moreover, Paul's lack of success had made him discouraged, so much so that he decided to forget the Jews and focus on the Gentiles. In frustration he cried, "Your blood be upon your heads! I am clean. From now on I shall go to the Gentiles" (v. 6). Yes, that is the same Paul that once said he would be willing to die for the salvation of the Jews.

Have you ever been defeated as a Christian witness? As a disciple? As a teacher? Have you ever said, "Forget it! These people are impossible! I'll move to greener pastures?"

Robert and Mary Moffat, mother- and father-in-law to David Livingstone, served as missionaries in one South African village for eight years. Seeing no one come to Christ, they changed their location and worked another four years; again without results. Their mission board prepared to call them home. It was felt that after twelve years with no fruit, Africa was a hopeless field. Just before they were to return home, a young man received Christ, then another, and before long a small church was formed. The Moffats were persistent, not wanting to give up, believing God wanted to work in Africa.

Paul wanted to close the door. But God said no. The Lord said to Paul one night in a vision, "Do not be afraid any longer, but go on speaking . . . for I am with you . . . for I have many people in this city" (vv. 9-10). That encouraged Paul to keep on. Assured that God was with him, he became bold. He persisted for eighteen months teaching the Word. And verse 8 says that eventually many believed and were baptized. Yes, Paul argued for the faith.

But secondly, *Paul built up the church.* Verse 23 says that he strengthened the disciples wherever he went. How?

First, Paul taught the Word of God to them, day in and day out. And secondly, he *lived* with some of the Christians and encouraged them by his life. Verse 2 says that Paul lived with Aquila and Priscilla. Aquila and Priscilla are a fascinating couple. They were Christian Jews who were deported from Rome in A.D. 49. Under an edict by Emperor Claudius, all Jews were expelled, probably because of a religious riot over the Messiah.

Rather than check in at the Corinthian Hilton and stay to himself, Paul lived alongside those Christians with the goal of building them up. That is always the best method of disciple-making. People can see if what you have really works. After traveling with Jesus all over Palestine, His disciples concluded that Jesus' message was trustworthy. Aquila and Priscilla must have concluded the same about Paul. They spent much time with him. Chapter 18 tells us that Paul *found* Aquila and Priscilla; he *went to see* them; he *stayed with* them; he *worked with* them; he *taught* them; he *traveled with* them to Ephesus; and finally, he *planted* them there to build the Ephesian church.

So, Paul the discipler did two things: he argued for Christ, and he built the church. The torch he carried was the light of Christ. He passed it on by persuasion and encouragement.

THE SECOND RUNNERS

But several runners carry the Olympic torch. They pass it on from one to another. So let us look at some of those who received the torch. Surely Aquila and Priscilla are prime examples. They are our second runners.

The New Testament does not tell us much about Aquila or Priscilla, but what it says is instructive. Aquila was a Jew from Pontus, near the border of modern-day Turkey and the Soviet Union. Priscilla was a Gentile from Italy, probably a noblewoman. For some reason, after being deported from Rome they ended up in Corinth. Perhaps they were expanding their business.

In Romans 16 Paul calls Aquila and Priscilla "fellow workers" in Jesus Christ who "risked their necks" for him. What that involved is uncertain. But you can be sure that they were some of Paul's closest friends.

The first clue to their characters comes in verses 24 and following. Aquila and Priscilla were in Ephesus. Paul had moved on. Then the brilliant Alexandrian Jew, Apollos, appeared on the scene. He came to the synagogue and preached of the coming Messiah of whom John the Baptist and the prophets spoke. Now watch Aquila and Priscilla go to work.

We said that two marks of disciple-makers are that they persuade others to the faith, and they build the church. That is exactly what Aquila and Priscilla did. We can probably assume that it was Paul who showed them how.

We first encounter them, as disciples, contending for the faith. They were in the synagogue worshiping when all of a sudden the silver-tongued Apollos began to preach. It is not that they disagreed with Apollos and had "roast preacher" for dinner. On the contrary, they agreed with him but believed that he did not yet know the whole story.

Apollos did not know that Jesus had died and risen. Apollos had not yet heard about or received the Holy Spirit. All he had was the Old Testament and the witness of John. He spoke about

Jesus' life but not about His finished work on the cross. W. A. Criswell likens his message to the truncated gospel of liberal theologians. They preach Jesus as our example but not Jesus as our Savior. They offer a reformer but not a Redeemer.

Aquila and Priscilla were impressed with Apollos. But they were burdened to show him the gospel in its fullness. Verse 26 says they "took him" and "explained to him the way of God more accurately."

Now Apollos was skilled in rhetoric. He knew his Old Testament backward and forward. And for him to accept all that Aquila and Priscilla said probably took a lot of persuading. But the two disciple-makers argued and argued well. For in verse 28 we see Apollos preaching the gospel as Aquila and Priscilla knew it.

So, first of all, Aquila and Priscilla contended for the faith. But secondly, like Paul, they built up the church by their encouragement.

Notice, they did not denounce Apollos for his incomplete preaching. They took him—probably invited him to dinner—and helped him. Then, along with the rest of the church, they encouraged him and wrote a letter of commendation that he could take with him to the churches in Greece (v. 27). Would that our churches did that when believers move their membership.

Aquila and Priscilla also encouraged by opening their home. What examples of Christian hospitality! As refugees in Corinth, they opened their home to Paul. As missionaries in Ephesus, they took in Apollos. In fact, 1 Corinthians 16 says that, in Ephesus, they opened their home as a meeting place for the church. Then later, when they moved back to Rome, Romans 16 says they had church meetings in their house there as well.

This adventurous couple Paul called "co-workers." As a man and a woman together involved in the mission of the church, they let go of the nesting instinct that many couples have and went where the Spirit of God prompted. They had a pilgrim mentality. They opened their possessions to others. They were willing to risk coffee spilled on the carpet and broken dishes by letting their house be used for the Lord.

These two were a disciple-making couple. They took others

in, handed them the torch of the gospel, and sent them out to pass it on.

THE THIRD RUNNER

But our chapter mentions a third runner in this relay of the gospel. Paul trained Aquila and Priscilla. Aquila and Priscilla trained Apollos. And now Apollos wishes to leave for Achaia to pass the gospel torch there as well.

What is said about Apollos should not surprise us. Like Jesus and Paul, he too was a disciple-maker. Verses 27-28 show Apollos doing two things. First, the text says, he powerfully confronted the Jews in public, showing by the Scriptures that Jesus was the Christ. He had an argument. He argued for the light. And secondly, the text says, he greatly helped those who had believed.

So we have seen three generations of disciples in action. No wonder the gospel spread so fast. And because of what we find here as the typical pattern for making disciples, we have to ask ourselves, What kind of disciples are we? Are those two marks of disciple-makers evident in our own lives?

You may say to yourself, "But wait a minute, I'm not a minister!" But you are! In the New Testament, it is never one man who does all the work. Paul says it is *the saints* who do the work of the ministry. And so we must ask ourselves, What is the argument of our lives? You might not be a professional apologist, but your works and actions argue for something. Our lives speak one message or another.

My wife's father and mother were bakers. They had a bakery in Dillenburg, Germany, and, after emigrating, in Fairlawn, New Jersey. As bakers, they had a unique advantage in advertising. They had no need to run ads. All they needed to do was open the door and let the aroma draw people in. Your life gives off an aroma. What kind is it? Does your very manner contend for Christ?

We must ask what kind of influence we are in the church. We are influential. We either build up or tear down. What about you? Paul was known for strengthening Christians by his teaching. Aquila and Priscilla did it in more common ways—by words of encouragement, by hospitality, by letters of commendation.

A Christian is by nature a disciple of Jesus. And all disciples have a commission that is yet to be fulfilled: we are to be disciple-makers. Jesus commanded, "Go . . . and make disciples of all the nations." And He gives twentieth-century disciples the same comfort that He offered Peter, John, and Paul—that He will be with us always, "even to the end of the age."

Remember

There are two activities that are crucial for disciples: contending for the faith and building up the church.

Paul lived with some of the Christians and encouraged them by his life.

Aquila and Priscilla encouraged others by opening their home.

Your life gives off an aroma. What kind is it?

A Christian is by nature a disciple of Jesus, and all disciples have a commission that is yet to be fulfilled.

Questions

1. What two activities are crucial for disciples and why?
2. What is it that made Aquila and Priscilla a fascinating couple?
3. How did Aquila and Priscilla deal with the incomplete teaching of Apollos?

Assignment

Analyze your own life. Are you presenting a positive witness for Jesus Christ? Determine specific ways you can be an encouragement to other Christians, and begin to implement them.

Acts 19
The Trap of Idolatry

We easily fall into idolatry, for we are inclined to it by nature.
— Martin Luther

Idolatry. It sounds like an old-fashioned word. Mention idols, and our minds conjure up primitive statues being worshiped by half-naked savages. Mention idols, and we think of the gods of ancient Greece and Rome or grotesque figures from the Orient. Mention idols, and you may even recall the golden calf worshiped by Israel when she forsook Jehovah.

The Bible's picture of idolatry may surprise you. Of course we find the obvious idolatry of paganism. As Paul entered Athens, he saw the city was "full of idols" (17:16). In Romans 1, Paul says that men rebelled against God and worshiped images in the forms of men, birds, four-footed animals, and crawling creatures. Yet that is only one type of idolatry.

The Scriptures picture idolatry in a broader sense. Writing in Colossians 3, Paul calls "greed" idolatry. In 1 John 5, John warns believers to keep themselves from idols. John is probably thinking of false spirits, false prophets, and false teaching. If we look back into the Old Testament, we even see the prophet Ezekiel warning Israel against taking idols into their hearts.

It seems that in those passages "idolatry" has moved beyond the physical worship of graven images. Therefore, a biblical definition of idolatry should include anything claiming that loyalty of our hearts that properly belongs to God alone. With Scripture defining idolatry as such, it is as relevant to twentieth-century man as it was to ancient man.

Acts 19 portrays the apostle Paul in a head-to-head confrontation with the idolaters of Ephesus. It is one of the great "battles of the gods" in Scripture. Like Isaiah before him, Paul argues that there is no god like the one, true God, the Father of our Lord Jesus Christ. All other contenders he calls "no gods."

In this chapter we want to reconsider the subject of idolatry: its influence and challenge in both Paul's day and our own.

THE OLD IDOLATRY

Acts 19 finds Paul in the setting of the great commercial city of Ephesus. He was on his third missionary journey. Paul probably devoted more time to ministering at Ephesus than any other city except Rome.

In this chapter we find three characteristics of the Ephesian idolatry.

We are first confronted with its awesome proportions. If you were to book a week-long tour of Ephesus in Paul's day, you would probably visit the famous temple to the goddess Artemis (or Diana). That temple was magnificent. It was one of the seven wonders of the ancient world. Some said its beauty surpassed the other wonders, including the hanging gardens of old Babylon, the statue of Olympian Zeus, the Colossus of Rhodes, and the pyramids of Egypt.

The temple itself was four times as large as the Parthenon, making it the largest temple in the ancient Greek Empire. It was surrounded by 127 columns that were beautifully sculptured at their base. Pliny said that the temple took 220 years to build. To many in Paul's day, it appeared to be an immortal structure. Acts 19:27 says that its reputation as a center of worship extended throughout the world.

A second characteristic of Ephesian idolatry was its obvious physical nature. Worship was given to visible images. Inside the great temple was a statue of Artemis. There she was portrayed as a woman with many breasts, symbolizing her ability to nourish the earth. She was a goddess of nature and fertility. The people claimed that the statue of Artemis had fallen from the sky. As such, it was endowed with miraculous powers. She could do everything from healing the sick to regulating the economy.

The religion of the Ephesians exerted so much influence that the people devoted one entire month of the year to honoring her. During that time business stopped. Days were spent in amusement reveling around the annual athletic games. There were also wild orgies, feasting, and carousing. Thousands of worshipers and spectators attended, many from other Asian cities.

A third characteristic of Ephesian idolatry was economic—it was big business. Acts 19 says that craftsmen associated with the temple generated great wealth. City jewelers selling statuettes of the goddess and her shrine made fortunes. Demetrius the silversmith was one such craftsman. He appeared as the head of the temple union, rallying his fellow craftsmen together when their profits came in danger.

Alongside that souvenir industry, some scholars believe that the temple even contained a bank with all the business typically associated with banking. Is it any wonder that the Ephesians were upset when Paul came preaching a message that threatened their business?

So three characteristics seem prominent in the worship of Artemis: it was an awesome enterprise, it was blatant physical idolatry, and it was a lucrative religion.

As an apostle of Christ, how did Paul respond to all that? He reacted in three ways:

First, he *confronted* idolatry. Paul faced it and warned believers against its more subtle forms. He did not run away from the challenge, nor did he disown the Ephesians as hopeless pagans. Rather, he confronted the situation. He penetrated the culture with the light of the gospel, just as he did in Athens and Corinth.

Second, Paul responded to the idolatry by *opposing* it. One can address a situation and yet never clearly speak one's mind. Man has a tendency to compromise or accommodate. We do not know what the synagogue in Ephesus did as it put up with the idolatry. Perhaps it retreated. Maybe there was minor accommodation. But Paul opposed it head on. He took a stand.

As he preached of the one true God and His Son, people began confessing Jesus as Lord. "The word of the Lord was growing mightily," says verse 20. People involved in the magic arts left their occult practices. They publicly burnt their occult books as a witness to their new Lord.

In fact, God used Paul's preaching to reach such great numbers that the craftsmen of the city began to worry. Led by Demetrius, they plotted how to rid themselves of the Christian troublemaker. Evidently, Paul's preaching had an impact. He told people that the entire cult of Artemis was a hoax, and that there is only one God.

Verse 27 shows the response of the craftsmen to his message. They said, "Not only is there danger that this trade of ours fall into disrepute, but also that the temple of . . . Artemis may be regarded as worthless and that she . . . should even be dethroned from her magnificence." Deposed by whom? By Paul and the gospel of Jesus Christ.

Men do strange things when someone threatens their checkbooks. In Ephesus, the craftsmen gathered together in the theater and for two hours shouted "Great is Artemis of the Ephesians!"

The Old Testament gives precedence for Paul's opposition to Artemis and the idolatry of his day. Through the prophet Isaiah, God opposed idolatry in Israel, saying, "To whom would you liken Me?" Those who made and worshiped gods of wood, gold, and silver were fools. Those gods cannot move. They do not answer. They are unable to save anyone in trouble. Then God declared, "I am God, and there is no one like Me" (Isaiah 46:5, 9).

The text of Acts is clear: Paul, as a prophet, not only confronted the idolaters of Ephesus, but he also opposed them by his preaching.

A third way in which Paul responded to the ·idolatry in Ephesus is found outside the book of Acts, in Paul's letter to the Ephesians. He *admonished Christians to be on guard.* There Paul warns Christians against viewing idolatry as always forthright and physical; sometimes it takes a deceptively subtle form. Covetousness can be idolatry, he warns in chapter 5.

Aristotle Onassis once said, "All that matters in this life is money. It is the people with money who are the royalty in our generation." Ultimately he discovered that he had leaned the ladder of his life against the wrong wall. When he died, the only person at his side was his daughter; his money brought no comfort.

In essence, Paul says, be subject to Christ and not to desires for material things. The idolatry of worshiping Artemis is easy to identify. But Paul speaks of another, more subtle way of denying God. He writes that Christians should be on guard against idolatry of the spirit.

Looking at Paul and the idolatry of Ephesus from our own day, we face the temptation to pat ourselves on the back. After all, we are civilized, not naive enough to worship rocks and wooden images. We are modern. We are enlightened. We live in a technological society.

However, in spite of our sophistication, Scripture broadly defines idolatry. More than physical worshiping, idolatry wears many faces. That gives the first commandment a timeless relevance, which brings us to reconsider idolatry in a new setting —our own generation.

THE NEW IDOLATRY

On the surface, idolatry seems improbable in a nation where most people believe in God. The Gallup polls seem encouraging. But on a deeper level, there is cause for great concern. The polls overlook two kinds of modern idolaters.

The first kind say, "I believe in God" when in reality they believe in other things. They believe in the ladder of promotion more than the God of the Scriptures. They follow the god of security and material comfort. Maybe pursuit of the opposite sex has become their god. It may be career-making or power-grabbing. Food or drink may have enslaved them. Often, those people take as their god things that are not bad in themselves. However, they have gradually become everything. Have you placed something like that above the Lord God?

A second kind of modern idolater is the man whose creed

is atheism or agnosticism. His problem comes about because his mind and actions betray him. For in fact, he believes in *something* passionately. It is not my God. But it is certainly his.

Think of the secular humanist who believes not in God— but in man as the measure of all things. Think of the political religions of Nazism and Marxism. Think of those who look to science to usher in the millennial age, or those who bow to "progress." Consider the one taken in by the cults or the one who retreats to the old gods of paganism and regulates his life by the stars.

All of those objects of devotion have replaced belief in God. Those gods are not less divine because we print their names with small initial letters. Perhaps ancient man exhibited more honesty by capitalizing the names of their idols, by personalizing them, and by building temples to them. But those things do not confer divinity. Things become gods as we give them first place in our hearts.

Our age boasts of being a skeptical age, but in many ways it is a superstitious one. Polytheism lives! Idolatry has become subtle.

That is the main difference between the old idolatry and the new. The old was bold and obvious. But ours, marked by subtlety, is all the more deadly. The subtlety hides its magnitude in our society. We no longer have temples to Artemis. Today we build temples to the gods of oil, trade, insurance, and banking. The worship is more discrete but every bit as lucrative. Idolatry has possibilities today of which the priests to Artemis never dreamed.

So how must a Christian respond to modern idolatry? Notice Paul's response to the idols of his day.

First, Paul *confronted* them. And so must we. The deceptiveness of modern idolatry makes our task more difficult. Rather than separating from the pagan world, we must realize that God has set us in the world as light and as salt.

Paul did not confront pagan Ephesus with an army and a guard campaign. He did not speak of strategies to "impact" culture, as some Christians do today. Instead, he lived obediently as a Christian man. He preached the gospel in word and deed as he lived among the Ephesians.

Second, Paul *opposed* idolatry where he found it. Like Jesus, he made a definite judgment. In Matthew 6:24 Jesus says, "No one can serve two masters. . . . You cannot serve God and mammon." The word *mammon* there means "money" or "profit." To say that we can serve money personifies the word and makes it a lord. Jesus says that no one can combine devotion to the Lord God with devotion to the lord mammon. Jesus opposed that lord, just as Paul opposed Artemis. And likewise, Christians must oppose the idols of the present age.

Opposition takes many forms. Paul preached with his words and life. But he also argued and exposed the weakness of ancient idols. They were "no gods." Time has proven Paul right. The site of Artemis's temple today is a stagnant pool of dirty water. The same fate awaits the gods of our age. And like Paul, we can assist in knocking the idols off their pedestals.

Finally, Paul *admonished Christians to be on guard*. The slide into idolatry is easy. Our task then is to be subject to one Lord—the Lord Jesus Christ. Walk with Him and draw near to Him, for He alone is Lord. That was the confession of the early church. May we confess the same and live for Him each day.

Remember

A biblical definition of idolatry should include *anything* claiming that loyalty of our hearts that properly belongs to God alone.

Paul warned Christians that idolatry is not always forthright and physical. Sometimes it is deceptively subtle.

Idolatry wears many faces. That gives the first commandment a timeless relevance.

Idols may be things that are not bad in themselves but which have gradually taken first place in a person's life; they have been placed above the Lord God.

Perhaps ancient man was more honest by capitalizing the names of their idols, by personalizing them, and by building temples to them.

162 The Acts of God

Luther said, "We easily fall into idolatry, for we are inclined to it by nature."

Questions

1. How does the Bible picture idolatry?
2. Describe the characteristics of idolatry as it was found in the worship of Artemis (Diana) at Ephesus.
3. In what ways did Paul war against idolatry?
4. Describe the main difference between the idolatry of the ancients and contemporary idolatry.
5. Give some examples of modern-day idolatry.

Assignment

Analyze your own life. Is there anything that has taken the place of the Lord God? If so, bring it before God and confess it as idolatry. Then place Christ back on the throne of your life.

Acts 20
A Biblical Definition
of Leadership

We need a baptism of clear seeing. We desperately need
seers who can see through the mist—Christian leaders with
prophetic vision. Unless they come soon it will be too late
for this generation. And if they do come we will no doubt
crucify a few of them in the name of our worldly orthodoxy.
— A. W. Tozer

I have often said that if you do not have a goal, any road will get
you there. Without goals we flounder.

Occasionally, in helping students define their goals, I advise
a little creative writing. "Compose a few paragraphs about yourself for *Who's Who*," I suggest. "Describe the person you want to
become and the achievements to which you aspire." I even tell
them to write their own obituary! "Explain how you would like
to be remembered by your friends and the world in general."

Life-definition is crucial to life direction. A definition, or
goal, streamlines our thoughts. As we review it, it teaches us to
say yes to some things and no to others.

If ever there lived a man of definition it was Paul of Tarsus.
As a Pharisee he excelled beyond his peers. As a persecutor he
tracked the church as a lion tracks its prey. As an apostle of
Christ he ranked second to none.

In Acts 20 we find Paul's definition of Christian leadership.
Returning from his third missionary journey, he calls the elders
of Ephesus to meet him in the port city of Miletus. There he

gives them a final charge so they might have an ideal to aim at as church leaders.

You will remember that Paul had been planting churches throughout Greece and Asia Minor. Since his conversion he had only one goal: to fulfill his ministry. And now in an informal meeting with the elders of Ephesus, he challenges them to fulfill their ministry as well.

Churches who are without pastors and thinking about leadership will find Acts 20 a marvelous chapter. Pastors taking an inventory of their ministry will find a gold mine of information. Paul's words carry a message for all believers hoping to fulfill their ministry. He uses here a series of four words to define Christian leadership.

SERVING

The first word to appear is *serving*. A Christian leader serves. In verses 18-19 Paul says, "I was with you the whole time, serving the Lord with all humility and with tears and with trials."

Periodically, Christians, and especially church leaders, must ask themselves, "Who are we really serving—God or man?" Let's face it: our egocentric natures are incredibly anxious to dethrone God's rule in our lives. Our living sacrifice crawls off the altar. To our secret self we say, "Mine is the kingdom, and the power, and the glory forever and ever."

Paul rejected the way of self. He steadfastly served God. When threatened with imprisonment or attacked by the mob, he did not do what comes naturally and try to save his skin. He counted his life as nothing compared to the honor of serving God. He never compromised his loyalty in serving the Lord.

But you may ask, How did Paul serve God? Our text says that Paul served God *with humility*. He not only claimed to be a servant, he displayed the attitude of a servant as well. He imitated Christ, who humbled Himself by being obedient to the point of death. In verse 24 Paul says, "I do not consider my life . . . as dear to myself, in order that I may finish my [ministry]."

Paul not only served with humility, but *with tears and trials*. What made Paul weep? Elsewhere in the New Testament we find that Paul wept over false teachers (Acts 20:31), carnal Christians (2 Corinthians 2:4), and lost people (Romans 9:2-3). The theology of his head touched his heart.

D. L. Moody exhibited the same concern of the heart. British pastor R. W. Dale once said that of all the preachers he had ever heard only Moody was qualified to preach on hell. For Moody could not get far in his preaching until the tears began streaming down his cheeks.

Paul served God like that. He served with "many tears."

But Paul also served with many trials. His life was literally a danger zone. Verse 19 shows the Jews plotting against him. Chapters 21-28 show that plot thickening. Paul moves from one courtroom to another defending himself against false accusations.

Paul set as his goal in ministry to serve the Lord, and service to God meant trials.

In Medieval Europe, some Christians believed it a sign of deep spirituality to pray for the marks of Jesus to appear on their hands and feet. One story tells of a monk who, while praying for those marks, received a vision. In his vision he saw another mark on Christ's body that the world had forgotten. It was the bruise-mark on His shoulder, which came from carrying His cross. The monk learned that he could only have the marks on his hands and feet if he first had the mark upon his shoulder.

In Galatians 6:17 Paul writes, "I bear on my body the brand-marks of Jesus." He served God at a cost. He suffered many trials. But it was all part of a task that had to be accomplished. Even today the cost of leadership involves suffering.

Yes, the word *serving* plays an integral part in Paul's definition of Christian leadership.

TEACHING

Paul next uses the word *teaching* as he defines Christian leadership. Verse 20 reads, "I did not shrink from declaring to you anything that was profitable, teaching you publicly and from house to house."

The *contents* of Paul's teaching centered in the Word of

God. Only there can we find a profitable word. In his letter to the Ephesians, written later in his life, Paul repeats some of the things he had taught them face-to-face. Acts 20:27 tells us that Paul taught the Ephesian Christians the "whole purpose of God." He gave them the meat of the Word after they had learned to swallow the milk of the Word. He helped them grow into mature, healthy believers.

Besides the content of Paul's teaching, we should also consider his *method*. Verse 20 says that he taught both publicly and from house-to-house.

Public teaching is no stranger to most of us. The teaching of the Word, alongside the sacraments and discipline, acts as an identification mark—a dog tag—so to speak, of the church.

But in our generation we often neglect the old practice of house-to-house teaching. Do not confuse such teaching with a "visitation ministry" or a friendly visit. This ministry actually took the teaching into people's homes. The teaching elders went where people lived: perhaps to house churches but more likely to families. Pastors would join a family's worship and then speak the Word to a specific situation. People find it easier to remember teaching at their doorstep than at the church step. Yet sadly, in our day, one rarely finds either family worship or a teaching ministry in the homes.

Beyond the content and method of Paul's teaching, we must not forget the *goal* of his teaching. In Ephesians 4 he tells pastors and teachers to equip the saints for the work of the ministry until all are mature in Christ. Paul accomplished that during his stay in Ephesus. He taught himself out of a job. He trained others to oversee the flock. That was his goal.

So, all along, we see Paul teaching. He lives like Jesus. He talked of Jesus, and he pointed to Jesus.

TESTIFYING

Besides *serving* and *teaching*, Paul uses the word *testifying* to define leadership. This is the act of preaching or sharing faith in Christ with others. Paul was a tireless testifier. Everywhere he went, he would preach.

John Wesley lived that way too. For fifty-four years Wesley

preached three sermons a day. Then, at age eighty-three, it bothered him that he could only preach twice a day. His age limited him to write no more than fifteen hours a day. He also complained in his diary that he could no longer rise as early as he used to. He now stayed in bed as late as 5:30 in the morning.

Verse 21 says that Paul testified to "both Jews and Greeks of repentance toward God and faith in our Lord Jesus Christ." Paul refused to become trapped in a Christian ghetto. He labored with Christians, but he witnessed to the lost. That balanced outreach kept Paul's ministry on the cutting edge. When he taught the church, his new converts reminded him of the reality of the power of Christ.

One of the problems we have today is a failure to maintain that balance. Believers huddle together. However, in reality, we need fellowship with the body *and* outreach to the lost. A body of water without a source of fresh water grows stagnant.

One of my four sons, while studying at a secular university, established what he called a fifty-fifty rule. He spent half of his extracurricular time working with the Christian fellowship; the other half he spent participating in student government. There he encountered the non-Christians. There natural witness took place. Perhaps such a rule would benefit you.

Paul was a man in the world though not of it. He was a man of the church but also an ambassador to the lost. He ministered in the key cities: Corinth, a trade center; Athens, an intellectual center; and Rome, an imperial center.

In those key cities of the ancient world he brought the gospel message of repentance and faith in Christ. He told men both the good news and the bad news. He told people they were rebelling against God in their hearts. They were fighting Him. They were sinning against Him by ignoring His laws. They needed to repent—to change their ways and admit their failure. They stood under God's judgment.

Notice that Paul believed there was a place for negative preaching. His message did not simply give positive affirmation.

Along with the bad news, however, Paul never failed to tell the good news. "Believe on the Lord Jesus Christ" he told the Philippian jailer, "and you shall be saved."

Paul habitually testified of his faith in the Lord Jesus.

COMMENDING

Finally, Paul uses the word *commending* as he defines Christian leadership. Verse 32 reads, "And now I commend you to God and to the word of His grace, which is able to build you up and to give you the inheritance among all those who are sanctified."

After serving well, after teaching and testifying well, God called Paul to another assignment. The work in Ephesus would be removed from his hands. Paul tells the elders, "You . . . will see my face no more" (v. 25). Then came the tears, hugs, and farewells. The elders walked Paul to the harbor where they put him on an outbound ship.

Commending marks Christian leadership because it recognizes that God calls us to specific tasks that can be finished. When God called, Paul had to let go of Ephesus. Leaders find that difficult. By nature they like to be involved in the details. The temptation is to do it all themselves. But not Paul. He "let go" after faithfully training the elders of Ephesus. Then he prayed and committed them to God's care.

In fact, Paul claims in verse 26 that he is innocent of their blood. If they failed, the fault would not lie with him. He trained them carefully. He could leave the Ephesian church without regrets. He accomplished all that he set out to do. Now he could return to Jerusalem with the great satisfaction that he had made a lasting spiritual investment in the people of Ephesus.

In 1920 Cecil Rhodes, the famous British financier, neared death. Rhodes had amassed a fortune in mining diamonds and gold in South Africa. Expressing remorse at the end of his life, he said, "I've found much in Africa—diamonds, gold and land are mine, but now I must leave them all behind. Not a thing I've gained can be taken with me. Eternal treasures that abide I have not sought; therefore I actually have nothing at all." Rhodes died with regrets. He never accomplished all that he hoped, and too late he discovered that he had invested in the wrong commodity. Little remained to commend.

How different from the life of Paul. Paul invested in people. That is what church leadership is all about. Our work can be finished with no regrets. If you will be serious about serving God, He will be serious about using you. Second Chronicles 16:9 says, "For the eyes of the Lord move to and fro throughout the earth that He may strongly support those whose heart is completely His."

Paul's heart belonged completely to Him. What about yours? Paul could write at the end of his life, "I have fought the good fight, I have finished the course, I have kept the faith; in the future there is laid up for me the crown of righteousness, which the Lord, the righteous Judge, will award to me on that day; and not only to me, but also to all who have loved His appearing" (2 Timothy 4:7-8).

Will you fight the good fight? Will you finish the course? Then *serve the Lord, teach, testify,* and *commend* until He comes again.

Remember

Our egocentric natures are incredibly anxious to dethrone God's rule in our lives.

What Paul did during his stay in Ephesus was to teach himself out of a job. He trained others to oversee the flock. That was his goal.

Paul was a man in the world though not of it. He was a man of the church but also an ambassador to the lost.

Paul believed that there was a place for negative preaching. But along with the bad news he never failed to tell the good news.

Commending is a mark of leadership because it recognizes that God calls us to specific tasks that can be finished.

Questions

1. Describe those marks that characterized Paul's service.
2. What was the content, method, and goal of Paul's teaching?
3. What importance did Paul place on testifying?
4. Why is commending an important part of leadership?

Assignment

Take the four key words that define Christian leadership for Paul and study how they fit into the lives of men like Moses or Elijah.

Acts 21
A Tenacious Faith

Faith, as Paul saw it, was a living, flaming thing leading to surrender and obedience to the commandments of Christ.
—— A. W. Tozer

How few are the lovers of the cross of Jesus." So wrote Thomas a Kempis nearly 560 years ago in his classic *The Imitation of Christ*. The world usually misunderstands those, like Thomas a Kempis, who love the cross of Jesus.

According to Paul, those raised on Greek wisdom viewed the cross as foolishness. The Romans accused early Christians of being morbid in their focus on the crucifixion. "Why rejoice in the death of a victim?" they asked. Christians have always answered, "Because the Victim became the Victor." The crucified Christ became the risen Lord.

Faith enables people to see beyond the agony of the death of Jesus. The cross was no hapless streak of bad luck that fell upon a virtuous teacher. It was a divine appointment to deal with the problem of human sin. When Jesus set His face toward Jerusalem, He was ready to offer Himself as a sacrifice for our sins. In giving Himself, He broke the power of sin for us. Death could not hold Him. Jesus Christ arose from the dead.

The cross became a place of new beginning. That is why Christians shout about it. We place an empty cross on top of steeples and sometimes wear them on our lapels or around our necks.

But the faith of Christians not only looks beyond the cross, it enables us to endure a cross. Knowing that Jesus set the example, martyrs gladly marched into Roman arenas to be devoured by lions. Knowing that Jesus passed through death triumphantly enables believers to risk everything for Him.

Paul's life illustrates that kind of faith. Paul was a lover of the cross of Jesus. In Acts 21, he sets his face toward Jerusalem, ready to die for Jesus' sake. Paul was no fool. He saw death as a passageway—either a dungeon door that led to eternal separation from God, or a celestial door to the kingdom of God. In Christ, Paul did not fear death; he welcomed it. By faith, he willingly risked everything in life for everything in death.

Examine the faith of Paul for a moment. In Acts 21 we read of his travels from Asia Minor to Palestine. The Holy Spirit of God compelled him to return to Jerusalem. Yet all along the way his friends discouraged him from going. "It's too dangerous," they said. "You'll be captured and imprisoned," they warned. Ignoring their words, Paul continued on.

What led Paul on? How could he apparently give up common sense and walk into a sting operation arranged by his enemies? What kind of death was it that led Paul on?

Acts 21 shows us Paul's tenacious faith. In these verses and in the rest of Acts, we see its three characteristics.

PAUL POSSESSED AN OBEDIENT FAITH

Paul knew God's will. It led him to return to Jerusalem. Already in 19:21 we see that "Paul purposed in the spirit to go to Jerusalem." Again in 20:22 he says, "Bound in spirit, I am on my way to Jerusalem."

The fascinating thing about Acts 21 is that Paul's friends opposed him. When he stopped at Tyre, the disciples warned Paul not to go on.

When he came to Caesarea the prophet Agabus confronted him. He approached Paul, took Paul's belt, and with it, bound his own hands and feet. Then he warned the apostle, "This is what the Holy Spirit says: 'In this way the Jews at Jerusalem will bind the man who owns this belt and deliver him into the hands of the Gentiles' " (v. 11). When the other disciples heard that warning, they urged Paul to change his plans. Luke says, "And when we heard this, we as well as the local residents began begging him not to go up to Jerusalem" (v. 12).

The two conflicting claims about the will of God caused a problem. The disciples said, "Don't go." But Paul himself felt compelled to go. According to Luke, the mistake lay with the disciples. Although they correctly understood the information about what would happen, they mistook a prophecy of hardship and imminent suffering as a sign that God did not want Paul in Jerusalem.

Does all that raise questions in your mind? How can we know the will of God if even the advice of Christian friends can be wrong?

In *How to Discover the Will of God*, I encourage four things: To know God's will we must first accept God's salvation in Christ. It is God's will that none should perish. Second, to know God's will we must be obedient to God's Word as recorded in the Scriptures. We find 90 percent of God's will right there. Third, to know God's will we must pray and earnestly seek His direction. Fourth, to know God's will we must listen to the voice of the Holy Spirit.

Paul followed those basic guidelines. Yet in spite of the danger and risk, Paul responded, "I am ready not only to be imprisoned, but even to die at Jerusalem for the name of the Lord Jesus."

Paul determined to obey the Spirit, regardless of the circumstances. Therein lies the difference between Paul and the other disciples. They looked to circumstances alone to discern the will of God—clearly the wrong path. God calls us to walk by faith. Had Abraham chosen the way of sight, he would never have believed God to open Sarah's womb. Had Jesus solely considered His execution, He would have avoided the cross. The path He took was not the obvious path of a Messiah. It was a path discerned by obedient faith, not sight. When Paul wrote his epistle to the Corinthians he put it just this way, "For we walk by faith, not by sight" (2 Corinthians 5:7).

The only course open to Paul, then, was obedient faith. Unlike Jonah, Paul obeyed God's will. When God told Jonah, "Arise, go to Nineveh the great city, and cry against it, for their wickedness has come up before me" (Jonah 1:2), we read that Jonah fled to Tarshish from the presence of the Lord. Jonah disobeyed the voice of God. He had not yet learned the lesson of obedient faith. He looked at circumstances. He disliked the Ninevites and feared a hostile reception, so he ran from the situation.

How unlike Paul. As chapter 21 proceeds, we see that Paul did arrive in Jerusalem. He could not tell what awaited him —perhaps death. Paul went to Jerusalem by faith, obedient to the Spirit's command. Paul possessed an obedient faith.

PAUL POSSESSED A SUFFERING FAITH

Paul willingly obeyed even with the probability of persecution. In Acts 20:22 he says, "I am on my way to Jerusalem, not knowing what will happen to me there, except that the Holy Spirit solemnly testifies to me in every city, saying that bonds and afflictions await me."

Yes, Paul walked into suffering service with a tenacious faith. He willingly went through anything because he believed God. He knew that beyond suffering waited glory. So he became a lover of the cross of Jesus.

Thomas a Kempis did not see many people like that in his own day. He wrote:

> Jesus hath now many lovers of his heavenly kingdom, but few bearers of his cross. He hath many desirous of comfort, but few of tribulation. He findeth many companions of his table, but few of his abstinence. All desire to rejoice with him, few are willing to endure anything for him. Many follow Jesus unto the breaking of bread; but few to the drinking of the cup of his passion. . . . Many love Jesus so long as adversities do not happen. Many praise and bless him, so long as they receive comforts from him. (*The Imitation of Christ* [Chicago: Moody, 1980], pp. 114-15)

That rings true today.

The Christian faith is a suffering faith, and we must not forget it. Notice three ways suffering comes to Christians.

By persecution. Paul wrote to Timothy, "Indeed, all who desire to live godly in Christ Jesus will be persecuted" (2 Timothy 3:12). To the church at Philippi Paul wrote, "For to you it has been granted for Christ's sake, not only to believe in Him, but also to suffer for His sake" (Philippians 1:29). Jesus said to His disciples, "Because you are not of the world . . . therefore the world hates you" (John 15:19). The New Testament clearly tells Christians to expect suffering in persecution.

By bodily decay and death. The Bible says that it is appointed unto all men once to die. Our human body begins to deteriorate early in life. Paul says that "the whole creation groans and suffers" (Romans 8:22). In 2 Corinthians 5:2 he says that as long as we remain in this body we will groan. Face up to it: we live in a fallen world; Adam's sin infects all of creation; the wages of sin is death.

In the growth of their Christian lives. This aspect of the gospel receives little attention these days. Growth includes pain. We forget that. Sometimes we are so growth-oriented, so overindulged with "abundant life," that we lose sight of true Bible theology. The life of Christ promises both "abundant life" and suffering. Remember that Jesus taught His disciples to die to themselves. Believe me, in my life that involves pain. Jesus said we must lose our lives in order to find them. That also requires pain. In Colossians 3:5 Paul says, "Put to death therefore what is earthly in you." That also means suffering.

The sacraments of the Christian church remind us of the importance of suffering to the Christian life. In baptism we pledge to live a pattern of dying to self and living in Christ. In the Lord's Supper we see the body and blood of the Lord Jesus.

The Christian life involves suffering. A suffering-free Christianity is a hoax. It does not square with the New Testament. And yet it is popular in our day.

One best-selling religious book claims that "You can have exactly what you want, when you want it, all the time." Such advice is nonsense and finds no place in Jesus' teaching.

Paul calls us to realism—to a sober-minded biblical realism. As long as we live in this world, suffering should not surprise us. Expect it.

But let us also balance the account. For Scripture abounds with promises. Paul knew this. Such promises sustain a suffering faith. The psalmist writes, "Many are the afflictions of the righteous; but the Lord delivers him out of them all" (Psalm 34:19). In Jesus we are promised an exodus, a way out paved by the cross. God's Son entered our hopeless situation and defeated the powers of death and decay. His cross gives us the promise of strength for today and bright hope for tomorrow. The resurrection frees us from these weak decaying bodies. We will have new bodies, resurrection bodies. There will be no more disease, no more hunger, no more oppression, no more moral decay.

But besides the promises of deliverance, Scripture also reminds us of the present opportunities in suffering. James writes, "Consider it all joy, my brethren, when you encounter various trials, knowing that the testing of your faith produces endurance. And let endurance have its perfect result, that you may be perfect and complete, lacking in nothing" (James 1:2-4).

Our trials become God's opportunities. Paul knew that only suffering can teach some of His most important lessons.

I have now had two bouts with cancer. Both involved extensive radiation treatments. In these difficult hours, I sensed God's refining work. In suffering I became a better lover of His cross.

Suffering teaches. It is essential to faith. So it should not surprise us to learn that Paul's faith was a suffering faith.

PAUL POSSESSED A VICTORIOUS FAITH

Paul's faith was not only an obedient faith and a suffering faith but a victorious faith. You will not find this in chapter 21. You must read on to discover the end of Paul's story. In Acts 21 Paul does not know what will happen to him. Nevertheless he was ready to die in Jerusalem. Like Job, Paul's attitude was, "Though He slay me, I will hope in Him" (Job 13:15).

However, eventually Paul saw that God was far from being finished with him. God would use him to bring the gospel to imperial Rome.

The other disciples urged Paul to avoid Jerusalem and save his life—to preserve himself for effective ministry. Had they intervened, Paul would have probably had many opportunities in the regions that he had served in his previous missionary outreach. But God had something else in mind. God planned to bring the gospel to the capital city of the Roman Empire.

Acts 22 through 28 chronicles Paul's journey from one ancient courtroom to another. In each one he gives a defense that includes a clear presentation of the gospel. He testifies before the crowd, and then before the Jewish council and the high priest. He makes a defense before various rulers: Governor Felix, Governor Festus, and King Agrippa. Finally, Paul's appeal brought him into the court of Caesar.

Although our records are incomplete, most scholars believe that Paul was freed in Rome and had several years of ministry there. Some think that he even traveled to Spain.

Can you see how much life came to a man willing to lay down his life? Can you see how greatly Paul loved the cross of Jesus?

Jesus gave His life so that we might really live—that we might have life more abundantly. The faith He placed in His Father was obedient faith, it was suffering faith, and it was victorious faith. It overcame the world.

Paul followed his Savior and Lord. He had a tenacious faith. His eyes were not ultimately on the world. They focused on God's kingdom. He recognized life as very short. He knew that it is not worth saving, not at the price of losing it in eternity. Have you placed your confidence in Paul's Lord?

Remember

Paul saw death as a passageway—either a dungeon door that led to eternal separation from God, or a celestial door to the kingdom of God.

We find 90 percent of God's will recorded in the Scriptures.

Paul willingly obeyed even with the probability of persecution.

"Jesus has many lovers of His heavenly kingdom, but few bearers of His cross. He has many desirous of comfort, but few of tribulation" (Thomas a Kempis).

178   *The Acts of God*

The Christian life involves suffering. A suffering-free Christianity is a hoax.

Questions

1. What four principles are important in discovering the will of God?
2. What dangers are there in relying on circumstances to determine God's will?
3. In what ways might suffering come to Christians?
4. Describe how Scripture balances suffering.

Assignment

Find one situation in your life (start out with just one small area) and determine to follow God whatever may result. Then follow Him wholly and completely, trusting Him to help in periods of suffering.

Acts 22
The Challenge of Closed Doors

Opportunities multiply as they are seized; they die when neglected.

— Unknown

An Irish boy roamed the hills outside his village. The path he followed led to a tall gate. He found the gate locked, so there was no going through. It hung on a high stone wall, and he could not go around it. He either had to give up his journey or figure out a way to climb over it. To build incentive, he threw his much-loved hat over the wall.

Then using his Irish common sense, he creatively found a way to get over, retrieve his hat, and continue his journey. The closed door had forced him to consider another way of accomplishing his purpose.

In Acts 21 Paul's ministry came to a screeching halt as he faced the wall of Roman arrest. Paul was beaten, seized, and bound. His missionary activity came to a standstill. However, he did not quit. Instead, he looked for new ways to compensate for the challenge of a closed door.

Acts 21-22 present three events that led Paul to redirect his ministry: his capture, his defense, and the response of his listeners.

PAUL'S CAPTURE

First, let us review the events of Paul's capture. The end of Acts 21 records them.

Paul's capture marks a closed door. His freedom to move as he pleased has disappeared. His time to spend with the Christians in Jerusalem is ended. He has no more time to be with friends and relatives, no more time to preach in the synagogues, no more time to visit the churches in Asia Minor. The door of a free ministry has slammed shut.

Do you recall how the disciples in Jerusalem begged Paul not to go to Rome? They feared that all his good work would come to an end. Now with Paul's arrest it seemed that their worst fears were realized.

One day while Paul worshiped in the Temple, some people from Asia, visiting Jerusalem for the Pentecost celebration, falsely accused him: "Men of Israel, come to our aid! This is the man who preaches to all men everywhere against our people, and the Law, and this place; and besides he has even brought Greeks into the temple and has defiled this holy place" (21:28). Those were serious charges. Were they true?

The accusation that Paul brought a Gentile into the inner court of the Temple is doubtful. The penalty for such an act was death, and Paul knew that. And according to what we read in chapter 21, Paul made every attempt to appease the Jews. It is therefore unthinkable that he would commit such an offense.

The other charges present more interest. They are familiar charges. Do you recall the story of Stephen in Acts 6? The Jewish leaders charged Stephen with speaking against the law and the holy place. In truth, however, Stephen spoke against neither. Rather, he emphasized that God cannot be confined by a Temple made with human hands.

Look again at the story of Jesus when He was charged with speaking against the Temple. They said that Jesus had spoken of destroying the Temple and rebuilding it in three days. Of course, Jesus spoke not about the Temple building, but rather the Temple of His own body. And elsewhere, when accused of speaking against the law, Jesus responded by saying, "I did not come to abolish [the law] but to fulfill [it]" (Matthew 5:17).

Now the same charges are thrown at Paul. But here too they are false. In the book of Romans, Paul calls the law holy and good. In Acts 21, we find him worshiping in the Temple. The indictment does not stand. It was the corruption of the law that Paul opposed.

Paul had no time to defend himself against the mob. They attacked him and dragged him out of the Temple. They even tried to kill him. By human standards, Paul's life and work seemed over. But God's work through Paul was not yet finished.

Have you ever had a door slam in your life as with Paul, where God either brought or allowed some difficult experience? Well, look at what happened.

Right before his arrest, Paul could not preach openly about Jesus, because hostility ran too deep in the Temple precincts. Only after his ministry in freedom ended did a new ministry in captivity begin—a new door opened.

The people beat Paul and drove him out of the Temple. Luke says that "all Jerusalem was in confusion" (21:31). Roman soldiers rushed in, trying to restore order. They arrested Paul, mistaking him for an Egyptian rabble-rouser who had disrupted the city in times past.

Leading him up the steps away from the angry crowd, the Romans finally realized that they had the wrong man. At that point Paul asked the soldier in charge if he could speak to the crowd. He received permission.

Here we have an amazing turn of events. Before his arrest, Paul had to keep a low profile and could not preach openly. Now in chains with the protection of Roman soldiers on each side, he could safely address the crowd. And that he did. God allowed one door to close, and when Paul looked around he found a new door opening up.

PAUL'S DEFENSE

Knowing something about the closed door of Paul's capture, consider the open door of his defense, described in the first twenty-one verses of chapter 22. Paul now begins his last address. Actually he gives them the testimony of his life. He tells of his upbringing, his education, his zeal as a Pharisee, his persecution of Christians, his meeting with Jesus on the Damascus road, and his mission as an apostle.

Chapter 22 is a masterful illustration of what one man did with an open door. Under tough circumstances, Paul shows us how to handle the open door of evangelism. Four principles of Christian witness stand out in Paul's defense.

First, Paul *identified with his audience*. He addresses them as "brethren and fathers," and goes on to say, "I am a Jew, born in Tarsus of Cilicia, but brought up in this city, educated under Gamaliel, strictly according to the law of our fathers, being zealous for God, just as you all are today" (vv. 1, 3). Paul so identified with them that he said he could understand why they would want to beat them. For the same reason, Paul himself used to hunt down Christians.

Second, Paul *talked to them in a language they understood*. He spoke in a Hebrew dialect and got their attention.

One need not compromise the message while putting it into contemporary language. This should be an aim of both evangelists and theologians: to state eternal truths in a modern setting with language that can be understood. Too often we forget that, because we are tempted to hang on to traditional ways of saying things for bad reasons.

For the same reason Luther received severe criticism when he translated the Bible into the language of the German people. Many could not understand Latin. German, on the other hand, communicated; the Word of God could be understood as a living Word and not a dead letter. Paul communicated in the language of the people.

Paul *simply shared what Jesus had done in his life*. Paul's life had drastically changed after meeting Jesus. He simply told his audience how it happened. He avoided engaging in heavy theological discourses. Verse 15 says that he witnessed about what he had seen and heard.

The blind man in John's gospel did the same when Jesus restored his sight. Unable to answer the Pharisee's detailed questions about the nature of Jesus, he simply replied, "Whereas I was blind, now I see" (John 9:25).

Paul told the crowd that what he once had been doing —persecuting Christians—was wrong. The door of his old life was closed. He was a new man. He had met the resurrected

Christ, who offered to forgive his sins and give him a new mission in God's service.

What about you? Can you witness to what you have seen and heard of Jesus in your life?

Paul brought his testimony of Jesus' work in his life up-to-date. Not merely a story of twenty years previous, he testified of God's present work in his life.

Fourth, Paul *pressed for a decision.* Either they were for the work of Jesus or against it. He ruled out fence-sitting. Paul said that God called him, not to minister in Jerusalem, but to minister to Gentiles beyond Jerusalem. He implied that in Christ those Gentiles found equal spiritual footing with the Jews.

Paul refused to go out of his way to be offensive. He simply wanted everyone to know that the gospel was for all people.

Unfortunately, his audience failed to accept that. Paul touched a tender nerve in his listeners. They interrupted him and never allowed him to answer their charges. Yet Luke records enough here to show us that Paul made good use of a splendid opportunity to witness about Jesus. When one door shut, he saw another door opened, and he boldly entered and shared the gospel.

THE RESPONSE OF PAUL'S LISTENERS

Luke records two responses to Paul's message in this passage: the response of the crowd and the response of the Roman commander.

The Jewish crowds rejected Paul and his message. In rejecting the gospel, the door of God's gracious offer of salvation to those people was closing.

Earlier in the story, the crowd had responded by trying to put Paul to death. After his speech, the crowd again lashed out. "Away with such a fellow from the earth, for he should not be allowed to live!" they cried (v. 22). Verse 23 says that they waved their garments and threw dust into the air.

Notice again that when Paul preached, there was usually a revival or a riot. Rarely did his audience remain neutral.

Years ago I submitted a cartoon to the *Saturday Evening*

Post. It pictured the apostle Paul attending a Monday morning pastors' meeting. The pastors were all dressed in their finest ministerial attire. By contrast, Paul looked in a bad way. His hair was disheveled, his tunic torn, and there was dirt on his brow. Gazing on the other clergymen, Paul said with surprise, "Where in the world did you preach yesterday?" Paul often created a stir.

In chapter 22 Paul's preaching stirred the crowd to frenzy. They treated Paul much like the crowd treated Jesus. In both instances they cried, "Away with him." They had no time for God's servant. They were anxious to get rid of Paul. They rejected the offer of God's Son. Sadly, a door was closing—the door of God's mission to Israel. From there on, the Spirit's activity focused on the Gentiles. There was unprecedented hunger for the gospel in Gentile lands. A grand new door was opening to the early church, and to Paul, in sharing Christ with those living far beyond Palestine.

But Acts 22 records another result, the response of the Roman commander. Rome stationed soldiers in Jerusalem to maintain civil order. They were the governing power in Palestine. They broke up the mob as it tried to murder Paul. In fact, they protected Paul as he spoke. Before they would allow the Jews to kill Paul, they wanted to know if his offense warranted death. So they took him to a safe place where the truth of the situation could be decided.

Of course, Rome had its share of corruption too. We see how the commander attempted to make Paul talk by ordering that he be scourged. Roman soldiers would take a whip of leather straps to which small pieces of metal were attached, and beat their prisoners until they talked.

But just before the whipping began, Paul wisely asked his torturers if it was right to whip a Roman citizen who was uncondemned. The answer was no. In fact, it was a crime to do so. The guards were shocked to learn that Paul was born a Roman citizen. Hurriedly they unchained him. Then they gave Paul another opportunity to defend himself before his accusers, the Jewish council.

Do you see the open door? When the door of his freedom closed at his capture, a new door opened with new opportunities. And when that door shut, another door of opportunity opened. Then another and another until Paul finally testified before the elite of Israel, many governors of Rome, and eventually mighty Caesar—all because of a closed door.

Paul faced some pretty dramatic closed doors in his lifetime. What do you face today? Sometimes a door will slam on a job. Sometimes it will slam on a ministry, like Paul's.

Sometimes doors will slam on a dream. Some have dreamed of excelling in vocations outside of the church, and then God called them to preach. D. L. Moody sold shoes. Martin Lloyd-Jones practiced medicine. As a boy I wanted to be an artist. But God called us all to preach. He closed the doors of our first profession. But new doors opened.

Others have dreamed of becoming preachers or pastors, and God said no to that. Them He called to be witnesses in business, at the factory, in the shop, or in politics.

Sometimes a door will slam on our health. John Calvin was a sick man most of his life. He called his body "an idiotic body" because it did not function normally. And yet God used that theologian in a marvelous way throughout church history to give definition to our faith and Christian life.

Consider the example of Joni Erickson Tada. Her handicap has allowed God to use her in ways that she had never dreamed of.

Sometimes God shuts the door of life itself.

But if you remember one thing today, remember this: in the will of God, a closing door marks a new opportunity. Ultimately, the Christian never finds himself in a room with all the doors closed. Even in death you have a new opportunity—eternal life with Jesus. Jesus said, "I am the door; if anyone enters through Me, he shall be saved, and shall go in and out, and find pasture" (John 10:9).

Remember

By human standards, Paul's life and work seemed over. But God's work through Paul was not finished.

God allowed one door to close, and when Paul looked

around he found a new door opening up.

This should be an aim of both evangelists and theologians: to state eternal truths in a modern setting with language that can be understood.

Not merely a story of twenty years previous, Paul testified of God's present work in his life.

In the will of God, a closing door marks a new opportunity. For the Christian, there are no rooms where all the doors are closed.

Questions

1. Explain the charges brought against Paul.
2. Compare Paul's opportunities to preach before and after his arrest.
3. What four principles can be learned from Paul's defense?
4. What steps did Paul take to make certain the people understood his message?
5. Why was the crowd so anxious to get rid of Paul?

Assignment

Identify some of the doors that have been closed on you. Determine your response to those closings. What other doors has God opened in their stead?

Acts 23
The Safest Place in the World

The history of all the great characters of the Bible is summed up in this one sentence: They acquainted themselves with God, and acquiesced His will in all things.

— Richard Cecil

An old gospel song by Elisha Hoffman ends with the refrain "Leaning, leaning, safe and secure from all alarms; leaning, leaning, leaning on the everlasting arms."

That old song brings home the truth that ultimate safety has nothing to do with seat belts, insurance policies, security councils, or natural vitamins. The Bible says, "It is appointed for men to die once" (Hebrews 9:27). No human invention can prevent death.

That song also reminds us that life on earth, besides being short, is fragile. Relations can go bad. Engines malfunction. Weather turns deadly. Bodies decay. Disease strikes. Children are abducted. Economies fail. Minds snap. Wars erupt. Read any responsible news magazine or history text and you will discover that in this world no ultimate safety can be found. A sickness called sin infects our earth. The world, the flesh, and the devil are very much with us. We walk out of step with God's original rhythm and purpose.

For that reason Christians ultimately think of security in terms of their eternal relationship with Jesus Christ. We affirm in the Apostles' Creed, "I believe . . . in the resurrection of the body, and in the life everlasting." Yes, we are to be responsible in this world, but we trust the risen Lord and have the absolute assurance that the dead shall be raised.

What is the safest place in the world? For the Christian, it is in the path that follows our risen Lord—the will of God. Paul followed that path. The assurance of the resurrection enabled him to live through the most trying circumstances.

In Acts 23 Paul is being pursued by his accusers. They are out to take his life and try to trap him legally. When that fails, they consider an ambush. Yet Paul, in doing the will of God, is perfectly safe and secure through it all.

Elsewhere, Paul explains his view of life when he says, "For to me, to live is Christ, and to die is gain" (Philippians 1:21). You see, Paul knew that the safest place in the world was in the will of God. In life, that meant living for the risen Christ. In death, it meant entering into His presence and having a resurrected body.

As we consider "the safest place in the world," let us look first at Paul's accusers and second at God's care.

Acts 23 contains the second defense of Paul's court battle. In our last study, Paul offered a defense before the crowd. Now he stands before the Sanhedrin. In his first defense, Paul told of his conversion to Jesus Christ. Then he was interrupted by the crowd and not allowed to finish. To protect Paul, the Roman commander Claudius Lysias brought him to the barracks. The next day, in a closed session with the high priest and the elite, Paul was given another opportunity to continue his defense.

Paul's Accusers

Paul's enemies relentlessly pursued him. They had two strategies for trapping Paul. First, they hoped to prove his guilt by trial. If that failed, then some of his accusers had a backup plan to take his life.

Look at their first strategy in Paul's trial. The trial includes two debates. The first debate involves Paul's conscience.

Paul opens his defense with a bold statement: "Brethren, I have lived my life with a perfectly good conscience before God up to this day" (v. 1).

Immediately, an amazing thing happened. The high priest, Ananias, commanded those next to Paul to strike him on the mouth. Paul could not believe that that would take place in a hearing before a Roman official.

Not aware of who ordered him struck, Paul responded in anger: "God is going to strike you, you whitewashed wall! And do you sit to try me according to the Law, and in violation of the Law order me to be struck?" (v. 3)

The official's action did not make sense to Paul. How could one legally try another and at the same time set aside the law? It was pure hypocrisy. Paul compared his accusers to an old, rotten wall covered with a fresh coat of paint.

Unknown to Paul, the man he called a "whitewashed wall" was the high priest himself. Upon discovering that, Paul immediately apologized, "I was not aware, brethren, that he was high priest; for it is written, 'You shall not speak evil of a ruler of your people' " (v. 5).

This first debate in Paul's trial is marked by great irony. Paul is being tried for law-breaking, for which he was not guilty. Then Paul tells the council that he has lived with a clear conscience before God. What did he mean?

On the Damascus road, Paul realized that it was wrong for him to persecute Christians. His statement about a good conscience therefore probably refers to his life since becoming a follower of Jesus.

How had Paul kept a clear conscience since his conversion? To answer this, we must first look back at chapter 22. There we see that Paul's good conscience began when he turned and followed the risen Christ. He was obedient to the Lord who met him on the way to Damascus.

Secondly, Paul kept a good conscience by listening carefully to the Holy Spirit. Chapters 20-21 demonstrate that, as Paul was "bound in Spirit" to go to Jerusalem.

Thirdly, in chapter 23 we see that Paul kept a good conscience by obeying the Scriptures. This short passage tells us a lot about who was keeping the law. Immediately, when Paul learned that he had insulted the high priest, he apologized, because he knew that the Scriptures forbid it.

Paul kept a good conscience by obedience to the risen Christ, to the Holy Spirit, and to the Word of God. That is the key to enjoying God's will. Jesus said that God's will consists of loving Him with all that we are. And elsewhere He said, "He who has My commandments and keeps them, he it is who loves Me" (John 14:21). Paul did not sit and wait for God to reveal all the details of his life in one grand blueprint. He discovered God's will by daily obedience to the written Word of God.

In contrast, look at the high priest. He pretended to abide by the law and to try Paul in a just manner. Then he interrupted the proceedings by demanding that Paul be struck. It seems that the high priest's character was not as law-abiding as one might have thought. He went along with the law only when it worked for his own ends.

This first scene clearly shows us who honestly cared for the will of God—Paul.

A second debate in Paul's trial concerns the resurrection itself. In an attempt to get down to basic issues, and in a display of foresight, Paul makes the point that he is being tried for his hope in the resurrection from the dead.

We have learned elsewhere in Acts that the Jewish council was split over the question of a general resurrection. The majority—the Sadducees—claimed it was impossible. There was no future life and no supernatural raising. The minority—the Pharisees—believed in things like the resurrection and angels. Now remember, Paul was a Pharisee. And seeing a splendid opportunity to bring the debate down to first principles, Paul very cunningly split the council so that they argued among themselves. He said boldly in verse 6, "Brethren, I am a Pharisee, a son of Pharisees; I am on trial for the hope and resurrection of the dead." At that, a great argument arose.

The scene would be comparable to that of a faculty member from the Moody Bible Institute going before the World Council of Churches and saying, "I believe in the infallibility of Scripture."

Not only would an argument arise—theologians love to dispute—but he would get pounced on as well.

Here in Acts the majority opposed Paul, for Paul believed not only in the resurrection from the dead, but in the resurrection of Jesus, which affirmed the general resurrection. The resurrection was crucial to all of Paul's thinking because he had met the risen Christ. That day on the road to Damascus, Paul had been stunned. The Christians were right!

After that time, Paul took on a resurrection mentality. He knew that life had significance beyond the material world. In chapter 24 he says there will be a resurrection of the just and the unjust. Paul realized that we gain safety on earth, not in saving our lives here but in losing them for Christ. He recognized Jesus was right. We do not gain safety by living for ourselves. Security comes only by dying to ourselves. The resurrection meant the extension of human existence. Paul stood for the resurrection and believed that a resurrected person was eternally secure. That was the safest place in the world.

You can imagine what happened. Debate between the Sadducees and Pharisees became so heated that the Roman commander moved Paul to a safer place, lest they tear him apart.

The courtroom strategy of Paul's accusers failed. Not surprisingly, someone brought up "Plan B." The second strategy, seen in verses 12-35, was to take Paul's life.

The plot is familiar. Men gathered to make an oath to kill Paul. Forty of them conspired with the aid of the high priest and planned an ambush. But a "mole" leaked the information to Paul and the Roman commander. Then Claudius Lysias ordered an escape by night. He gave Paul an armed escort and sent him to Caesarea, where governor Felix would try him. Claudius even mailed a letter to the governor explaining that Paul was not worthy of death.

You can almost see the surprise on the faces of Paul's accusers when they discovered that their plot had been ruined. And one feels for those poor men who vowed not to eat or drink until they killed Paul. Paul was safe, and they would have to wait a long, long time to satisfy their appetites!

God's Care

We have seen how Paul was pursued by his accusers. But now look at God's care of Paul. God kept Paul safe because it was not His will that he be killed. God had plans for Paul that no one could interrupt.

Verse 11 reads, "The Lord stood at [Paul's] side and said,

'Take courage; for as you have solemnly witnessed to My cause at Jerusalem, so you must witness at Rome also.' " Here again Paul meets the risen Christ and receives a promise of safe-keeping until he completes his assignment in Rome.

Paul was safe in the will of the risen Lord. There was no safer place in the world. And God had planned a trip for Paul—a trip to Rome.

When you plan a trip, what happens? Usually you have some inclination to go. You *want* to go. You dream of it. Then you confirm your desire with a reservation. Next you think about transportation. And finally, you might check into travel insurance.

Here in Acts we have an amazing thing. All along, Paul had a desire to preach in Rome. Now finally in chapter 23 Christ confirms it. Paul *must* go to Rome. And his travel was cared for courtesy of the Roman government. Travel insurance came in the form of a military escort. Imagine—two hundred soldiers, seventy horsemen, and two hundred spearmen!

Eventually Paul arrived in Rome. After some years of ministry there, he was martyred. And that is when Paul really started living!

Do not suppose that following Jesus Christ is always physically safe. I am not talking about physical safety but eternal safety. Remember, Paul was imprisoned and beaten along the way. He suffered with Christ in hopes of someday reigning with Christ. Paul's hopes were based on the promise of life in Christ Jesus.

No matter where you are in this world, safety is always tenuous. We do not know what can happen from day to day. The apostle James reminds us,

> Come now, you who say, "Today or tomorrow, we shall go to such and such a city, and spend a year there and engage in business and make a profit." Yet you do not know what your life will be like tomorrow. You are just a vapor that appears for a little while and then vanishes away. Instead, you ought to say, "If the Lord wills, we shall live and also do this or that." (James 4:13-15)

The Lord's will for Paul was that he obey Jesus Christ. There is true safety. Second Peter 3:9 says that "The Lord . . . is not wishing for any to perish but for all to come to repentance."

Will you repent of your sin and trust the One who was crucified and risen for you? Are you eternally safe? Or are you not sure where your life is heading?

I urge you to let go of your life so that Christ may have it. Lean on His everlasting arms. Get off the shifting sands of time and stand on the Rock of salvation. Open your life and receive the wonderful new life that is available in the Lord Jesus Christ.

Remember

Paul knew that the safest place in the world was doing the will of God.

Paul discovered God's will by daily obedience to the written Word of God.

The resurrection was crucial to all of Paul's thinking because he had met the risen Christ.

We do not gain safety by living for ourselves. Security comes only by dying to ourselves.

God had plans for Paul that no one could interrupt.

Do not suppose that following Jesus Christ is always physically safe. We talk here not of physical safety but of eternal safety.

Questions

1. What strategy was used against Paul in his trial?
2. Considering Paul's persecution of Christians, how and why could he say he lived with a clear conscience before God?
3. What is the key to knowing and being in God's will?
4. In Paul's reasoning, why was belief in the resurrection of Christ so important?

Assignment

Check your church library for a book on knowing God's will. Study its principles so you can better determine the path He has for you.

Acts 24
Where Is Justice?

Heaven is above all yet; there sits a judge/That no king can
corrupt.

— William Shakespeare

When I was a child in elementary school, we began each day
with the pledge to the American flag, the reading of a
psalm, and the reciting of the Lord's Prayer. The pledge to the
flag concluded with the phrase "With liberty and justice for all."
As we look at the world around us we sometimes ask, Where is
justice?

Ronald Eaton, charged for armed robbery, served a sixteen-
year prison sentence for a crime he never committed. After his
term ended and his innocence was proven, Eaton said, in retro-
spect, "Life played a dirty trick on me that day in the circuit court
of Rock Island, Illinois." Eaton asked himself the question,
Where is justice?

William Henry Alston of Maryland, an alcoholic, was arrested, incarcerated, and then placed in a mental hospital on
charges of breaking and entering. After months of treatment, authorities determined that they too had the wrong man. A journa-
list with the *Washington Post* who reported the story again
posed the question, Where is justice?

For Eaton and Alston, life took a tragic turn. According to
them, they did not get a fair shake. For many others in our world
it is the same way. Think of the small farmer or the slave. Think
of the nationalist Chinese. Think of the refugee and the raped
woman. Think of Paul.

Acts 24 pictures the apostle Paul cheated by both religious and civil law. He was stuck in a prison at Caesarea for two years while the Roman government ignored his case. I can almost hear Paul asking the same question: Where is justice?

Chapter 24 contains Paul's third defense in the court battle for his life. As he appeared before Felix, the Roman governor, a prosecuting attorney representing the Sanhedrin thundered out the charges against him. The truth was clearly distorted. Then Paul was allowed to answer. It seems the facts were on his side. But the governor was in cahoots with the Sanhedrin and would not set Paul free. Consequently, Paul would have to wait in prison for two years until Felix's successor offered a new hearing. There was little justice.

Paul knew what was happening. How could he go on? Acts 24 helps us answer that question.

MOCKING JUSTICE

First, see how the Sanhedrin mocked justice. In the courtroom, the lawyer Tertullus represented the Sanhedrin. Here are his charges: "For we have found this man a real pest and a fellow who stirs up dissension among all the Jews throughout the world, and a ringleader of the sect of the Nazarenes. And he even tried to desecrate the temple" (vv. 5-6).

There are four basic flaws in Tertullus's address. They reveal that he, like the Sanhedrin he represented, had no interest in justice. They mocked justice. They only wanted their victim —Paul.

First, consider how he flattered the governor, trying to score points through compliments. His praise of Felix was so excessive that it is a downright lie.

Tertullus said to the governor, "We have through you attained much peace . . . most excellent Felix" (vv. 2-3). However, that was not Felix's reputation at all. Historian Tacitus said that "Felix reveled in cruelty and lust and wielded the power of a king with the mind of a slave." Tertullus's words were only meant to flatter. Meanwhile, he conveniently failed to say anything about the governor's cruel and ferocious bite!

Next, consider Tertullus's distortion of Paul's arrest. Acts 21 records the facts of Paul's arrest. A riotous mob of Jews seized Paul and tried to kill him on the spot. Again the Romans saved Paul's neck and then arrested him. Tertullus, however, twists the facts to make the Jews look innocent and Paul look like a wild man.

Consider also the false accusation Tertullus makes in verses 5-6. Paul was called a pest "among all the Jews throughout the world." Moreover, he said that Paul profaned the Temple. In actuality, Paul was worshiping when he was arrested.

Finally, consider the lack of evidence. Tertullus had no witnesses. To properly condemn a Jew, he needed evidence of the crime. But, as Paul says in verse 13, they cannot prove their case. As with Jesus, "they kept trying to obtain false testimony . . . in order that they might put Him to death; and they did not find any" (Matthew 26:59-60).

So we have seen that the Sanhedrin's love of justice was imaginary. Their lawyer acted as if he were deeply concerned about truth. In fact, he tried to influence the judge by deceit and flattery; he distorted the truth of Paul's arrest; he made false accusations; and he spoke without supporting his claims. His case is shameful.

Tertullus, by his actions, despised the righteous standards of the God of Israel. He made a joke of the ninth commandment, which reads, "You shall not bear false witness against your neighbor" (Exodus 20:16).

DELAYING JUSTICE

What then of the Romans? The Roman Empire was famous for its laws, which were enforced throughout the ancient world. We can appreciate Rome's intention to keep the peace and to protect its citizens. But the system had its corruptions. Justice might have been upheld officially, but in Felix's case it was delayed.

After Paul finished his defense, Felix withheld his verdict until he could hear the testimony of Lysias, the Roman commander who arrested Paul. We can assume that Lysias eventually testified. But we find that Felix never issued a verdict' in Paul's trial.

Verse 27 says that Felix did not want to insult the Jews. He paid them a political favor at the expense of justice. So he delayed, and Paul spent two years at the mercy of an indecisive judge.

Part of Felix's delay, however, had nothing to do with favors owed to the Jews. Verse 26 says that, "he was hoping that money would be given him by Paul." In other words, Felix wanted a bribe. He was willing to be bought off by Paul. Perhaps he assumed Paul had wealth at his fingertips. He may have looked at Paul's citizenship as a sign that he had money. Maybe he figured that Paul's access to the reserves of the church could be his. Whatever his reasoning, Felix's motives showed. His delay for money and political favors tell us that he was a corrupt bureaucrat.

WAITING FOR JUSTICE

So far we have made two points: The Sanhedrin did not care about the law, for they mocked justice. And the Roman governor did not care about the law, for he delayed justice. Now finally, we find that Paul, the victim of this legal fiasco, waited for justice.

The only charge Paul was willing to admit to was that he worshiped the God of Israel as a Christian. But that was no capital offense. Paul's accusers had nothing on him. He was victimized by the system. He was trapped. There was no quick escape, so he waited for justice. But what did that involve?

First, it involved trust in God. Paul believed God's Word with all his life. When religious or civil law proved bankrupt, Paul did not dismiss their foundation. He did not become altogether cynical. Verse 14 says that his worship of God involved "believing everything that is in accordance with the Law, and that is written in the Prophets."

To understand Paul's trust in God's Word and law we must keep in mind verse 16. There Paul says, "I do my best to maintain always a blameless conscience both before God and before men." In other words, Paul's trust went beyond simple belief or a confession of the mouth; it included obedience—a confession of the life. Paul believed in God's justice. Of course, the Sanhedrin made the same claim, but Paul's life backed up his confession.

The Gallup Report on religion in America tells us that there is a religious awakening in our country. Most people believe in God. Many young people view the Ten Commandments as still valid for today. That is the good news.

But the bad news is this: Gallup concluded that religion has little influence on the morals of believers. There is little difference between the divorce rate or ethical conduct of Christians and non-Christians. The report concludes that religion is up, but morality is down. The survey also found the problem with young people. Although they believe in the validity of the Ten Commandments, few know what they actually are. Belief is shallow and cheap. In fact, it is often not belief at all. We call belief with the head and not the life hypocrisy. Trust involves an embrace by the whole person. Yes, while Paul waited for justice, he trusted in God and pursued justice with his life.

Second, Paul learned to wait patiently for justice. Paul knew that in God's time he would go to Rome. However, the delay required unusual patience. Imagine spending two years in prison waiting for justice.

Remember Joseph? After his brothers betrayed him and sold him as a slave, he ended up in Egypt as a servant to the captain of Pharaoh's guard, Potiphar.

Then Joseph was betrayed again, this time by Potiphar's wife. They threw him in prison. While there, however, he met Pharaoh's butler and baker. Joseph hoped that they might tell Pharaoh of his innocence.

But Joseph was betrayed a third time. Pharaoh's servant forgot to keep his promise. Joseph spent two long years waiting for something to happen. Genesis tells us that his only comfort was the presence of God.

Yes, like Paul, Joseph waited for justice, and he waited with patience. But it is tough to wait.

Third, Paul's wait for justice involved action. Paul always

made known the gospel no matter what the circumstance.

In Philippians 1:12-13, Paul writes this to fellow Christians, "Now I want you to know, brethren, that my circumstances have turned out for the greater progress of the gospel, so that my imprisonment in the cause of Christ has become well known throughout the whole praetorian guard and to everyone else."

Even in prison, Paul continued to preach. We find that in our chapter as well. After some days, Felix came with his wife Drusilla "and sent for Paul, and heard him speak about faith in Christ Jesus. And as he was discussing righteousness, self-control and the judgment to come, Felix became frightened and said, 'Go away!' " (vv. 24-25).

First Paul told of Felix's own rotten circumstances. Paul had perspective on the situation. His interest was in the soul of the Roman governor. So he told him of Jesus, the living Messiah, and that salvation only comes by trusting in Him. Look what happened then.

In the same session, Paul warned Felix and his wife about the cost of discipleship. Faith and grace were not cheap. Paul began applying the gospel to the lives of his audience.

Felix was told the very things he needed to hear. Paul told him about justice—an area that Felix had forgotten. Then Paul spoke about self-control. No doubt Felix and his third wife, Drusilla, had little restraint of their purse and passions.

You see, Paul's gospel was not "Five Easy Steps to Life." It called for repentance. It called for a new ethic. It was not a Sunday gospel. It was a workplace gospel, a bedroom gospel, a boardroom gospel, and a checkbook gospel. That shocked Felix. It demanded too much. He was alarmed. The cost was too high.

And fourth, Paul waited for justice with hope. That is obvious throughout Paul's defense. Verse 15 tells us that Paul had "a hope in God . . . that there shall certainly be a resurrection of both the righteous and the wicked." For Paul, the resurrection was crucial. To the one who trusts in Jesus as Lord and Savior it means a resurrection to eternal life.

There is, however, another side to the story. One other thing that Paul told Felix and his wife was that they had better prepare for a future judgment.

How often we forget that the same lips that articulated the Beatitudes and spoke the quiet parables told of a coming great and terrible day of the Lord. Jesus said, "Do not marvel at this; for an hour is coming, in which all who are in the tombs shall hear His voice, and shall come forth; those who did the good deeds, to a resurrection of life, those who committed the evil deeds to a resurrection of judgment" (John 5:28-29).

You and I will someday stand before almighty God to answer for our lives. Are your preparing for that day?

So often we act as if God is not there—as if our actions do not matter. No one is looking, so we cheat on our homework, avoid paying a toll, exceed the speed limit, falsify expense reports, withhold income tax, shade the truth to consumers, or talk behind someone's back.

Paul waited with hope. He did his best to maintain a clear conscious before God—to live according to God's law and to love justice. He knew that judgment was a fact of life, so he lived in light of that day. What about you?

As a young apprentice lawyer, Charles Finney sat in a village law office in New York. He had just begun his day; he was all alone. In the silence of the morning he began to question his ambitious career goals.

"Finney," a voice said, "What are you going to do when you finish your training?"

"Put out a sign and practice law," he responded to himself.

"Then what?" came another question.

He immediately thought, "Then . . . I'll get rich."

"And what then?" something inside him queried.

"Then I'll retire," his mind quickly answered.

"And then?" came the returning question.

"Die," he answered more slowly.

"Then what?" came the final question.

This time his answer came out with trembling. "The judgment!" was his hesitant reply.

When Finney turned his mind from a lucrative career in civil justice and considered the ultimate justice of God, he suddenly saw his life in new perspective. He saw himself at the judgment bar of the Almighty. His years of law school and the vanity of a selfish life immediately appeared empty.

Not long after that morning meditation, young Finney took time off to settle the question of his soul's salvation, and he found peace with God. His life was never the same. He became a great lawyer-evangelist and educator in the nineteenth century.

When you look at all the victims in this sinful world, the question is not, How can a loving God allow such injustice? but rather, How can a just God be so merciful and patient with me?

Where is justice? It is only partially manifest. But a day is coming when all accounts will be settled, when justice will neither be mocked nor delayed, when God will roll up history as a scroll, and the Just One, the Lord Jesus Christ, shall reign. The duty of the Christian until that time is to obey, patiently wait, and believe that, whatever happens, God is in control.

Remember

Paul waited for justice by trusting in God with all his life.

Paul believed in God's justice. The Sanhedrin made the same claim, but Paul backed up his confession with his life.

Paul knew that, in God's time, justice would be served and he would go to Rome.

Paul knew judgment was a fact of life, so he lived in light of that day.

Questions

1. What were the basic flaws in Tertullus's case?
2. What were the circumstances that caused a delay in Paul's case?
3. To which charge did Paul willingly admit?
4. Describe how Paul waited for justice to be served.
5. What did Paul tell Felix?

Assignment

Determine in which areas of your life you are asking, Where is justice? Write them down to help you define in your own mind the "injustice." Give them over to God and trust Him to settle accounts in His time.

Acts 25
Dead or Alive?

In the early 1920s, Nikolai Bukharin was sent from Moscow to Kiev to address a vast anti-God rally. For an hour he abused and ridiculed the Christian faith until it seemed as if the whole structure of belief was in ruins. Questions were invited. A priest of the Orthodox church rose and asked leave to speak. He faced the people and gave them the ancient Easter greeting, "Christ is risen." Instantly the whole vast assembly rose to its feet, and the reply came back like a crash of breakers against the cliff, "He is risen indeed."

— Source unknown

After stepping down from office, President Thomas Jefferson set out to write a significant book. He had long been troubled by the supernatural events of the New Testament. Yet he was enthusiastic about the moral teaching of Jesus.

Upon returning to his home in Monticello, Jefferson went to work with a scissors and a New Testament. He attempted to separate the "real" message of Jesus from all the "unnecessary." The final product omitted all references to the supernatural—including the resurrection of Jesus. The closing words of the so-called Jefferson Bible read, "There laid they Jesus, and rolled a great stone to the door of the sepulcher and departed."

For Jefferson, the resurrection was extraneous to all that Jesus was. His life story ended with death. Jefferson would have agreed with the Roman governor Festus in Acts 25. Festus, speaking to King Agrippa, also said that Jesus was dead. He believed that Paul's assertions of a risen Christ were mistaken.

In Acts 25, we find Paul's fourth defense. Again he stands

trial for obeying the risen Christ. Again, he is hounded by the chief priests and elders. And again, the Roman governor treats him unjustly. Paul endured all of that for his belief in the resurrection. In chapter 25 we learn that this trial was not merely a debate over a general resurrection. This debate centered on the resurrection of Jesus.

The chapter begins with Paul in prison and Festus taking over the governorship from Felix. Finally, Paul would gain a new hearing with a new governor.

It is not surprising, however, that the religious elite of Israel also approached the new governor to plot against Paul. They asked as a favor that Paul be sent from Caesarea to Jerusalem. They planned again to ambush and kill him.

Festus might have been a more respected governor than Felix, but his ethics were much the same. Verse 9 tells us that he wished to do the Jews a favor. Festus asked Paul if he would consent to moving the trial to Jerusalem. Paul said no; he was shrewd enough to know that once in the hands of his accusers he would be a dead man.

Seeing the governor influenced by the Jews, Paul made the ultimate appeal. Boldly he declared to the governor, "No one can hand me over to them. I appeal to Caesar" (v. 11). With that, Festus had no other option. He would send Paul to Rome. As a citizen, Paul had the right to appeal to the emperor himself.

About that time, King Herod Agrippa II came to Caesarea to welcome the new governor. Festus told the king about Paul's trial and asked the king to hear the case. But in Festus's summary of the trial, we learn how the debate over the resurrection had progressed. Verse 19 says that the Jews had certain points of dispute with Paul, about their own superstition *and* about Jesus, whom Festus asserted was dead but "whom Paul asserted to be alive."

Here we have two assertions over an extremely important issue: Was Jesus dead or alive?

Festus Said Jesus Was Dead

Festus claimed that Jesus was dead, a straightforward position. Yet it does not do justice to all of the facts.

We do not know how Festus backed up his case. But over the course of two thousand years we have heard his position many times. The old way of stating it said that dead men do not rise. A dead man is a dead man. Death's veto cannot be overturned, despite all of our hopeful protests.

But the assertion that Jesus was dead raises more questions than it solves. How do we explain the empty tomb? What transformed the despairing disciples into death-defying demonstrators of the Christian cause—men who turned the world upside down for their Master? In other words, what accounts for the dynamic origin of the Christian faith? Those facts must be explained before we can say, with Festus, that Jesus did not rise.

Various theories have been proposed, theories we can only sketch here but that are answered in detail elsewhere.

First, some suppose that *Jesus did not die on the cross*. After hanging on a cross, He fainted from exhaustion and loss of blood. Once placed in a cool, damp tomb He was resuscitated and eventually restored to health.

But a mortally wounded Christ would not unwrap Himself, roll away a stone that Mark calls "extremely large" (Mark 16:4), and overcome the Roman guard. Moreover, it is inconceivable that a wounded, weak Jesus could then turn the sorrow of His disheartened followers into a joy that caused them to worship Him as a risen Conqueror.

Second, some have suggested that *the disciples stole the body* after His burial and created legends of a risen Master to further their cause. But that theory also falls short of explaining how a group of men struggling with depression and cowardice could suddenly become so bold and optimistic shortly after the crucifixion. Besides, Christianity was not founded on deception. The apostles upheld lofty ethical principles. It makes no sense that they would base Christian teaching on a lie and then die a martyr's death for it.

Third, others have suggested that *hallucinations or visions* explain the resurrection appearances of Jesus. But more than five hundred people in various circumstances and of various states of mind cannot be deluded with the same vision. Those disciples not only claim to see Christ, but they claim to eat with Him and converse with Him over the course of many days.

206   *The Acts of God*

Fourth, still others suggest that *the disciples went to the wrong tomb*. But if that were true, the Jews and Romans could have easily produced the body and stopped the great storm of faith that arose in the early church. But they did not, because they could not find the body themselves.

Those are *old ways* of saying that Jesus was dead and that His body never rose. But there is *a newer* and more sophisticated way of denying the resurrection of Jesus' body. And surprisingly, some theologians promote it. First, they are extremely skeptical of the text itself, doubting its reliability. Second, they employ a form of double-talk—they affirm the meaning of the resurrection but deny its actuality.

All Christian theologians will say that "something happened" after Jesus' burial—they have to explain the church's explosive birth. And all Christian theologians will point to the resurrection as central to the faith. But one must probe further, asking what they mean by "resurrection." Is it a resurrection of the body? Was it His flesh that came forth—a transformed flesh, a glorified fleshly body?

Some theologians hedge on this point. They want the form of our faith but deny its power. They want the message of resurrection but deny the event. They want the hope of resurrection but not the fact. Indeed, one prominent German theologian says that "the resurrection of Jesus from the dead . . . does not speak the language of facts, but only the language of faith and hope."

There are problems with such skepticism and double-talk.

First, theologians misrepresent the text when they say that the references to the resurrection appear later in history and are therefore probably fictional. Paul wrote to the Corinthians that he delivered to them as of first importance what he also received. In other words, there Paul draws on the simple gospel as he first received it after his conversion. He received this: "That Christ died for our sins according to the Scriptures, and that He was buried, and that He was raised on the third day according to the Scriptures, and that He appeared to [Peter], then to the twelve. After that he appeared to more than five hundred brethren at one time, most of whom remain until now" (1 Corinthians 15:3-6).

Paul's belief in Acts 25 that Jesus rose from the grave is not a gospel reworked by Paul. It is the oral tradition that he received when he was converted and instructed by the other disciples. In other words, the material probably takes us back to five years after Jesus' death. Paul implies that the doctrine of a bodily resurrection has been there right from the start. It is no myth.

Scholars who affirm the resurrection idea but then deny its fact not only are unduly skeptical about Scripture, but they also resort to a theological double-talk foreign to the apostles. The man on the street does not understand that way of speaking; neither would the apostles' audience. Suppose the apostles held the same view as some of our liberal theologians. Suppose they affirmed the idea of the resurrection but denied the event; would their audience infer that from their writings and preaching? Of course not. And if their own audience could not pick up that meaning, it is because they were not meant to. The apostles were simple men who preached plainly. They knew that to use double-talk is no way to communicate. Rather, it misleads. It is an absurd device for someone who wants to put across a burning message.

If a man or woman assumes that dead bodies do not rise, then they have no choice but to approach the New Testament like Jefferson. They are naturalists. But if they think that it might be possible, if they suppose with Paul that God can do the impossible, then they will have to consider the second assertion in our chapter.

PAUL SAID JESUS WAS ALIVE

The second assertion found in Acts 25 is that Jesus is risen. Contrary to Festus and the Sadduccees, contrary to the skeptics, and contrary to the sophisticated theologians of today, Paul held to a bodily resurrection.

Paul reasoned something like this: Decay and death are elemental truths of biology, but the God who created the world can work with nature in any way He pleases. So Paul poses this question to his audience: "Why is it considered incredible among you people if God does raise the dead?" (26:8). He believed that flesh could be transformed. He knew that "acts of God" had not ceased. They were decisive in Israel's history. And if God brought forth a Son, then that would be a place supremely prepared for God to act again. Before his conversion, Paul, as a Pharisee, believed in a general resurrection. He was a supernaturalist. But he did not accept the Christian claim that Jesus rose. Jesus was an upstart who had been executed for throwing all Jerusalem into theological confusion. "Why would the Messiah suffer and die?" Paul thought. He was supposed to reign and lift Israel out of her bondage. According to the Old Testament, men who were crucified were accursed. They could not qualify for the title of Messiah, let alone risen Lord.

Paul set out for Damascus with one intention: rout the Christians and destroy their heresy. But when he met the risen Jesus on the Damascus road he realized that Christian belief was no heresy at all. What Paul experienced was not merely a vision. He fell to the ground. He heard a voice. He carried on a conversation. In fact, later in his ministry, Paul based his own claim to apostleship on the grounds that he had seen Jesus. Only an eyewitness had the right to be an apostle.

If Jesus were truly dead, Festus and his followers must tell us what changed hardened skeptics like Saul of Tarsus and James the brother of Jesus. What turned the cynics into inflamed preachers? Festus must tell us why the scattered disciples became sons of thunder. He must tell us how to account for an empty tomb and such a host of eyewitnesses.

Although it is important to show that Paul's assertion is reasonable, we must also understand why the resurrection played so central a role in Paul's theology. For Paul, the resurrection was *the* central fact of Christianity. It affirmed that God was truly in Christ. It pointed to the one place in history where death was decisively overcome. It showed that there is life beyond death. For Paul, that was the greatest miracle of Jesus. His resurrection tells us that there is a power greater than the world's sin. The real power of the universe is the power of the living God, which raises men from spiritual death, psychological death, social death, and physical death. Jesus' resurrection body gives us a vision of the Lord at work for us, bringing us God's forgiveness and redemption. It gives us a vision of the first material expression of the resurrection of all believers.

In 1 Corinthians 15:14-20 Paul highlights the importance of the resurrection, saying that if Christ is not raised, then we are really in a mess. Our preaching is in vain. We misrepresent Christ. Faith is futile. We remain in sin. At death we perish. If Christ is not risen, then death is stronger than God. Jesus is a lie. God's promises died with Him. Hope is empty. Paul says that if Christ is not raised, then "we are of all men most to be pitied." And later he adds, "If the dead are not raised, 'Let us eat and drink, for tomorrow we die.' " In other words, if death is final, then self-indulgence is our only course.

But Paul's life made him assert with confidence that death is not final. A resurrection is coming, and its first evidence is in Jesus.

Paul experienced the power of the resurrection when he met the risen Jesus on the Damascus road. There Paul found forgiveness for his past sin, power for living, and hope for the future.

We can experience the power of the resurrection today. The resurrection and the cross go together. Christ died in our place. He took our sins upon Himself. The righteous Son of God defeated sin's power. By trusting in Him we are asking Him to take our sins, and He promises in return to give us His resurrection. All that Jesus did for us in His death is confirmed in His resurrection. It is that great event that all men must reckon with.

The mausoleum on Red Square in Moscow is famous for displaying the embalmed body of Lenin. The pyramids of Egypt are well-known because they house the mummified bodies of ancient Egyptian kings. Mohammad's tomb is noted for the bones it contains. Westminster Abbey of London is a memorial housing the bodies of English heroes. Our own Arlington Cemetery in Washington, D.C., is the honored resting place of great Americans. All of those places are famous. They attract visitors because of the bodies they contain.

However, there is all the difference in the world between those monuments and the tomb of Jesus. Although pilgrims still come to Jerusalem, Jesus' tomb is famous because it is empty.

Christians assert that Jesus' bones are not there. He is risen from the dead.

Dead or alive? In the case of Jesus it makes all the difference in the world.

Remember

Festus said that Jesus was dead, a straightforward position. But it does not do justice to all of the facts.

Christianity was not founded on deception. The apostles upheld lofty ethical principles. It makes no sense that they would base Christian teaching on a lie, then die a martyr's death for it.

Paul's belief in Acts 25 that Jesus rose from the grave is not a gospel reworked by Paul. It is the oral tradition that he received when he was converted and instructed by the other disciples.

Paul reasoned something like this: Decay and death are elemental truths of biology. But the God who created the world can work with nature in any way He pleases.

If Jesus was truly dead, Festus and his followers must tell us what changed hardened skeptics like Saul of Tarsus and James the brother of Jesus.

Questions

1. What are the various "old" theories that attempt to explain Jesus' resurrection?
2. What causes each of those theories to fall apart?
3. Describe the newer way of denying the resurrection of Jesus' body.
4. How is it that some modern theologians try to hold that position?
5. What difference did it make to Paul whether Jesus was dead or alive?

Assignment

Make a chart showing the various theories used to explain Christ's resurrection and give scriptural references that show the fallacies of each theory.

Acts 26
Will the Real Madman
Please Stand Up?

If God spoke to man through Christ, then the most reasonable thing in the world is to listen and obey Him.
— George Sweeting

Many false accusations were hurled at the early church.
Some faced accusations of atheism because they accepted
Jesus Christ but rejected the gods of Greece and Rome. Others
were accused of polytheism because they worshiped the one
God as Father, Son, and Holy Spirit. Some Christians were accused of cannibalism because they claimed to eat Christ's flesh
and drink His blood. At the celebration of Pentecost in Acts 2
Christians are accused of drunkenness because of their expres-
sions of praise as they received the Holy Spirit.

In chapters 21-25 Paul answers the false accusations of the
Jews. The Jews called for the apostle's death on the grounds that
he was subverting their religious system.

In chapter 26, Paul must answer one last charge. But this
time the Roman governor Festus did the accusing. Paul had just
made his fifth defense in his lengthy trial. This time he reviewed
the facts before Festus and King Agrippa. Again, Paul told of his
startling conversion on the Damascus road, his devotion to the
risen Christ, and his commission to bring the good news to the
Gentile world.

Paul's trial then took a subtle turn. Like the trial of Jesus, the
original charges could not stand. In Acts 26, we find that the

original charges against Paul were groundless. Festus concluded that Paul had done nothing worthy of death. Appealing to an outside opinion, Festus asked King Agrippa to consider the case. Agrippa came to an identical conclusion: "This man is not doing anything worthy of death or imprisonment." King Agrippa then informed Paul that he "might have been set free if he had not appealed to Caesar" (vv. 31-32). In other words, even though the Jews persistently called for Paul's death, the original charges no longer stood.

The surprise of chapter 26, however, is the new charge hurled at Paul. This change came from Festus as he interrupted Paul's testimony: "Paul, you are out of your mind! Your great learning is driving you mad" (v. 24).

In reply, Paul protested, "I am not out of my mind, most excellent Festus, but I utter words of sober truth" (v. 25).

Paul and Festus had yet another disagreement. A chapter earlier, Festus claimed that Jesus was dead whereas Paul asserted that He was alive. Now Festus said that Paul was mad. Not able to handle the evidence of the case or Paul's argument, Festus attacked Paul personally. In defense, Paul claimed sobriety and truthfulness.

Who was right in the dispute over Paul's sanity? Had the apostle "gone over the edge" in his religious commitment? Or was Festus desperate to explain away Paul's defense?

Paul's words show how very sane he was. If anyone was mad it was the governor. Consider the following evidence.

PAUL TOOK HUMAN NATURE SERIOUSLY

We could hardly expect a sober, balanced judgment to come from the lips of a lunatic. But throughout Acts Paul describes human nature in careful terms. Remember his message to the Athenians? He quoted their poets and spoke of God as the One in whom we live and move and exist. We are "His offspring" (17:28). In other words, Paul believed that mankind was created in the image of God.

But that is only half the story, for in chapter 26 we see the other side of Paul's belief about the nature of man. Here he describes the human race living with closed eyes. They are in darkness because of open rebellion against their Creator. In verse 18 Paul reveals his purpose in preaching: "To open their eyes so that they may turn from darkness to light and from the dominion of Satan to God, in order that they may receive forgiveness of sins."

So Paul believed two things about human nature: it derived its dignity from the living God, but its selfishness came from man's rebellious heart. Both Paul and Jesus spoke of the estranged human heart—the heart of darkness. Jesus says in Mark 7:23, "Evil things proceed from within."

In our own age it is hard to find an analysis of human nature that is as judicious. Among philosophers and social scientists, we too often find theories that do not fit human experience. Sometimes man is reduced to the sum of his parts. That is the materialist's solution, which says man does not need salvation because he has no material soul. Materialism tells us that what man needs is to be remade by the social engineers, the behaviorists, and the genetic technicians.

Ordinary people cry out against that, for deep inside man knows he is greater than the sum of his parts. He has a soul. To reduce man to his organs is madness.

On the other hand, we find thinkers who go to the opposite extreme. They say man is not debased but divine. Man's problem is that his good nature is too often encumbered by bad environment. The need of man is more freedom. And so the quest for greater liberty. They give an admiring glance to the noble savages of the jungle. They imitate primitive art. Their educational system would teach children self-expression rather than submission to authority.

But again, most people know that our nature is not that angelic. The tension at home, the selfishness of the work place, the headlines of the daily paper, all remind us that something down deep is wrong. To ignore man's aggressive selfishness is also madness.

What about Festus the governor; what did he think? From all accounts, those issues were of no concern to him. Festus was the politician's politician. Like some modern bureaucrat, he

dealt with externals only. Spiritual things were, apparently, irre-
levant to his work. Like Felix his predecessor, Festus was a
wheeler-dealer—out for himself. For him, statecraft had nothing
to do with soulcraft. Rather, He was wielding power for Caesar.
He was solely concerned with the practical. He was the organiza-
tional man par excellence.

Who was mad? Not Paul! Paul took the great questions of
life seriously. He took man's divided nature seriously. If madness lay anywhere, it lay with Festus and with all those who refused to consider man as he really is.

Paul Took God's Salvation Seriously

Chapter 26 recounts the famous Damascus road experience. That may make Paul sound like a mystic—seeing visions
and hearing voices. Paul was supernaturalist but not a mystic.
You will remember that for a long time he refused to accept the
fact that Jesus was alive. Then one day, Paul's understanding of
God's work in the world was enlarged. On his way to raid the
Christian church in Damascus, he was thrown to the ground and
blinded. His life changed radically. Explaining away Paul's experience as epilepsy, hallucination, or psychological development
will not do. The text gives no indication of those.

The light of Christ that Paul was to share with the Gentiles
was the light that overpowered him on the Damascus road. It
was a light that opened his eyes to the spiritual side of life. It was
a light that brought about cleanness, wholeness, and forgiveness
of sins. He received it by faith in the risen Christ, not by the
works of religion. In verses 22-23 Paul reports the heart of his
message: "[I testify] nothing but what the Prophets and Moses
said was going to take place; that the Christ was to suffer, and
that by reason of His resurrection from the dead He should be
the first to proclaim light to the Jewish people and to the Gentiles."

In other words, Paul realized that man's fatal problem—sin
—needed a divine solution; and that solution was the life and
sacrificial death of God incarnate.

I can hear someone say, "But I don't understand this talk

about a death whose merits could be applied to others, and a body that could rise from the dead. It sounds unreal! Things like that just don't happen!" Such was the conventional wisdom of Festus.

But Paul knew better. First of all, Paul says in verse 8, "Why is it considered incredible among you people if God does raise the dead?" If God is God, Paul reasoned, then He may exercise His rights as Creator and Sustainer. He may act any way He pleases. That is not madness. It is perfectly reasonable. If God gives life, then He can surely raise life. If God can turn water into wine slowly on the hills of France, then He can surely speed up the process for a wedding in Cana of Galilee.

In chapter 25 Festus rejected the resurrection. To him all such talk was superstition. Many people in the world think like Festus. They claim to be against superstition, but usually they just exchange one so-called superstition for another. They do away with Jehovah only to set up a golden calf.

Festus had his own superstitions. Perhaps they were astrology or horoscopes, or omens and charms, or emperor worship, or any one of the mystery cults. Or possibly, Festus was a lot like modern rationalists. He seems to have prided himself in being a skeptic. Often, when skeptics debunk religion, they remove their trust in God only to place it in their own reason. Reason becomes their God, the judge of all reality. It tries to comprehend everything.

But is that sanity? Paul would contend that it is the height of madness. The Christian only claims to put his head into God's heaven. The rationalist attempts something even greater. He attempts to get the heavens into his head. Everything must be explainable by reason. But his head cannot contain the heavens. For the heavens are too grand. And so the rationalist's pursuit ends in madness. He attempts the impossible. G. K. Chesterton said that "the madman is not the man who has lost his reason. The madman is the man who has lost everything except his reason."

Christian belief in God's salvation is sane. As long as you have the salvation of a loving God you have health of mind. When you ignore that salvation, you are left with a crazy world.

The cross of Jesus Christ is the symbol of the salvation that God offers you. That cross is unlike the fixed and closed circle of reason. At its heart is the paradox of the God-Man. But its arms extend outward, opening to the whole world. Paul knew that. He staked his life on it. It is not madness to love the cross as Paul loved it. It is not madness to take God's salvation seriously. On the contrary, madness comes to those trapped in the confines of their own small minds and their dark rebellious hearts. Paul's sanity was verified by his view of God's salvation.

PAUL TOOK CHRIST'S COMMAND SERIOUSLY

If God has spoken to man through Christ, then the most reasonable thing in the world is to listen to Him and obey. We are speaking of God the Creator, who knows us better than we know ourselves. It is wise, therefore, to heed His word. We are speaking of God the Redeemer, who offers deliverance from sin and death. To ignore His outstretched hands is literally suicide, folly, and the epitome of madness.

Before meeting Jesus on the Damascus road, Paul knew something about taking God's command seriously. Consequently, he strove to be a Pharisee of the Pharisees! But after meeting Jesus, Paul saw God more clearly than ever before. Now he would have to take Christ's command seriously. His command to Paul is recorded more fully in chapter 26 than in the other two accounts of Paul's conversion (Acts 8 and 22). In verse 16 Jesus says, "But arise, [Paul] and stand on your feet; for this purpose I have appeared to you, to appoint you a minister and a witness not only to the things which you have seen, but also to the things in which I will appear to you."

Like all Christians, Paul was called to serve and testify of Christ. Christians have that common calling. Only our individual vocations differ.

In the eyes of the world a Christian witness in general, and a missionary calling in particular, is madness. The young Christian who is called to career missions or the pastorate, the middle-aged Christian who is called to abandon a career for the church, and the call to witness in a "secular" career; all make little sense to those in hot pursuit of the currency of our age.

Think of Spurgeon, who knew he was to preach as a young man. Think of the distinguished medical doctor Martin Lloyd-Jones, who left medicine to pastor a church. Or think of the great English don of Oxford and Cambridge, C. S. Lewis. Each of those men had an identical calling—to obey Christ's command, to serve Him, and bear witness to the Lord Jesus. Yet they were all appointed to different vocations. As each knew, serving Christ is the most important business on earth.

Not so with governor Festus. The Roman governor was involved in the enterprise of the *Pax Romana*, the Roman Peace. His pursuit was purely temporal. Festus did not realize that time was fleeting. The kingdoms of this world crumble. The nations are as a drop in the bucket. Paul was working for a lasting kingdom, and Festus was absorbed in a declining one. He was short-sighted, concerned only about his short span of government service and Rome's short dominance of the world scene.

People responded to Paul's life in a curious way. When they observed his pre-Christian life—ravaging the church, arresting Christians, and putting some to death—they did not accuse him of being mad. But when he gave all that up to serve Christ and bring the gospel to the Gentiles, only then was he accused of "excessive fanaticism." Festus and his friends across the centuries have dismissed him as a madman. Will the real madman of Acts 26 please stand up?

Writing to the Corinthians, Paul once said:

> Where is the wise man? Where is the scribe? Where is the debater of this age? Has not God made foolish the wisdom of the world? For since in the wisdom of God the world through its wisdom did not come to know God, God was well-pleased through the foolishness of the message preached to save those who believe. For indeed Jews ask for signs, and Greeks search for wisdom; but we preach Christ crucified, to Jews a stumbling block, and to Gentiles foolishness, but to those who are the called, both Jews and Greeks, Christ the power of God and the wisdom of God. Because the foolishness of God is wiser than men, and the weakness of God is stronger than men. (1 Corinthians 1:20-24)

Remember

Paul believed two things about human nature: it derived its dignity from the living God, but its selfishness came from man's rebellious heart.

If God gives life, then He can surely raise life.

Often when skeptics debunk religion, they remove their trust in God only to place it in their own reason.

As long as you have the salvation of a loving God, you have health of mind.

If God spoke to man through Christ, then the most reasonable thing in the world is to listen to Him and obey.

Questions

1. How did Paul describe human nature?
2. What is the problem with contemporary man's view of human nature?
3. What did Paul see as man's fatal problem? What was the solution?
4. Why is it sane to hold Paul's view of salvation?
5. What was the difference between Paul's obedience as a Pharisee and his obedience as a Christian?

Assignment

In light of this discussion of who really was the madman, analyze your own views of human nature, God's salvation, and obedience to Christ's command. To help solidify your thinking, write out a brief description of each.

Acts 27

A Confession
for a Stormy Day

The way we endure a crisis tells a lot about our faith.
— George Sweeting

On January 25, 1735, John Wesley was on board the British
vessel *Simmonds* bound for the New World. The destination was Georgia.

Two storms had already disrupted the three-and-a-half-
month journey. During one of them Wesley wrote, "The sea
broke over us from stem to stern, burst through the windows of
the state cabin . . . and covered us all over."

But the storm on January 25 was much worse. In the midst
of the turbulence, Wesley was dumbfounded by the abnormal
poise of a group of German missionaries. They showed peace in
the face of death. They said psalms while the waves crashed over
the ship, split the mainsail, and poured in between the decks.
The storm grew so intense, wrote Wesley in his journal, it was
"as if the great deep had already swallowed us up." Panic spread
among most of the passengers. But the Germans continued to
sing.

After the storm had passed, Wesley asked one of the Mora-
vians, "Were you afraid?"

The German Christian replied, "I thank God, no!"

"But were your women and children afraid?" Wesley persisted.

"No," the Moravian quietly explained, "Our women and children and not afraid to die."

As one historian observes, "His reply shook John Wesley even more than the storm had done."

The way we endure a crisis tells a lot about our faith. It indicates whether faith is a vital reliance on God or a fair-weather adornment.

In Acts 27 Paul and 275 other passengers endured a severe storm as they sailed for Italy. Paul was on his way to Rome to bring his appeal to Caesar. The storm was violent. It made the large wooden trading ship seem fragile. The crew, overwhelmed by the weather, despaired of their lives.

But in the midst of the tempest, Paul spoke with calmness. "Keep up your courage, men, for I believe in God" (v. 25). Like the Moravian missionaries on Wesley's ship, Paul displayed poise in the hour of crisis. He asserted with conviction his trust in God and His promise. He knew that God controlled the elements.

Paul's words remind us of the opening line of the Apostle's Creed—"I believe in God, the Father Almighty." Paul was not just reciting empty words or asserting a stale dogma reserved for moments of disaster. Instead, he spoke with deep conviction. For him it was a practical truth. The Lord God is sovereign over the most turbulent of circumstances.

Look closely at the nature of Paul's belief in God and the circumstances that tested his faith. Chapter 27 mentions three kinds of circumstances that draw out the nature of Paul's belief in God.

CIRCUMSTANCES IMPOSED BY OTHERS

Occasionally, others impose circumstances upon us. Sometimes we feel trapped because of what others do to us. We are forced into situations that we would rather not be in. It might have to do with a job, or an accident when the other person was at fault, or an awkward relationship.

Acts 26:29 has Paul still in chains. In verse 31, King Agrippa concludes that the entire trial had been a mistake. But Paul made an appeal to stand before Caesar, so the king and governor Festus respected Paul's right of appeal as a Roman citizen. They arranged for his travel to Rome.

Acts 27 has many reminders that Paul is at the mercy of others. The first verse reads, "And when it was decided that we should sail for Italy, they proceeded to deliver Paul and some other prisoners to a centurion of the Augustan cohort named Julius." Paul had neither voice nor choice.

Even the end of the chapter reminds us that Paul was a prisoner. As the ship hit a reef near Malta and began to break apart, verse 42 tells us that the soldiers were about to kill all the prisoners—even Paul—so that they might not escape. But for the centurion's intervention, Paul would have been dead.

Nevertheless, in the midst of such circumstances we find Paul resting in God's presence. In verse 23 an angel of God appears to him in the night telling him that he and the passengers of the ship will remain safe. Therefore, Paul says to his shipmates in verse 25, "Keep up your courage, men, for I believe God, that it will turn out exactly as I have been told."

As the seas churned and the winds howled, a transformation of Paul's status on board occurred. Paul the prisoner, who was formerly ignored by the others, became the man in charge. His moment came right when the rest of the crew began to despair. Verse 20 reads, "And since neither sun nor stars appeared for many days, and no small storm was assailing us, from then on all hope of our being saved was gradually abandoned."

At that point Paul spoke up: "Men, you ought to have followed my advice and not to have set sail from Crete, and incurred this damage and loss" (v. 21).

But he encouraged them: "I urge you to keep up your courage, for there shall be no loss of life among you, but only of the ship" (v. 22). In verse 31 he warns those sailors who were about to enter the dinghy and escape that they would die. At that point, they cut away the small boat and took Paul's advice. And finally, Paul encouraged them all to eat food for strength in the ordeal that awaited them.

We have seen it happen before in Acts: when Paul is bound, he is most free. Only after he is arrested in Jerusalem in chapter 21 does he find real freedom to preach—with Roman protection. In chapter 27, Paul the captive becomes Paul the prophet. He was the only one who had hope to offer in the storm. Now everyone listened to him.

Acts 27 again brings Joseph to mind. In all his unpleasant circumstances, Joseph maintained his integrity before God. He believed God, and God raised him up so that he became second in command of Egypt.

Paul, at the mercy of others, also reminds one of modern-day captives who have found freedom. Whether in a gulag or a state penitentiary, a Christian can be a free man. I have known men who, while serving a sentence, repented and trusted in Jesus Christ. Those men have become, in spite of the bars, some of the most liberated people on earth. They have become more free than their guards and wardens, more free than their captors, more free than those on the street who might be captive to their passions. Christ's reign in the heart transforms a captive man so that no circumstance ultimately tyrannizes him.

What about you today? Are you enslaved by conditions that others have imposed on you? Are you bound to a horizontal vision so that your captivity is all you see? Or do you have the upward look like Paul? Can you proclaim in your captivity the great confession of Paul? Can you say, "I believe in God," and rely upon Him as you sit in your chains?

CIRCUMSTANCES IMPOSED BY LIFE

Life also imposes circumstances upon the Christian, particularly in situations that arise in the cycle of life—situations of nature such as storms, shipwreck, and death.

Chapter 27 is a famous New Testament chapter, not only for what Paul says but also because of what it shows us of ancient seamanship. We have here details about a typical ancient merchant ship and how such vessels operated in inclement weather. But the rhythms of a boat on the Mediterranean Sea have something to say about the rhythm of life in general.

The voyage of Acts 27 began with the hope. In verse 1 it is the Romans who decided exactly what the destination would be. The journey started smoothly. But soon came the unexpected winds. Verse 4 says that "the winds were contrary," and verse 7 that the journey went slower than expected. And when they arrived at Crete, they arrived "with difficulty." They made a temporary stop in a port called Fair Havens. Verse 9 tells us that "the voyage was now dangerous since even the Fast was already over." The fast was the Jewish Day of Atonement. In A.D. 59, the Day of Atonement fell on October 5. That means the dangerous season for sailing had set in three weeks earlier.

The question then came before the crew whether they should stay in Fair Haven or move on to another harbor. Paul, a seasoned traveler, advised them to stay. In verse 10 he says, "Men, I perceive that the voyage will certainly be attended with damage and great loss." But Paul was ignored.

As the ship set sail again, a south wind blew gently (v. 13). That reassured the crew, and they supposed they had made the right decision. But then the tempestuous winds began to blow.

Like that ancient vessel, we begin our lives with hope of destination. A gentle wind often assures us that we are on the right course. But then come the contrary winds. Things go more slowly than we planned. Sometimes we ignore the advice of wise men like Paul. We then make bad decisions.

For the ship, things went from bad to worse. A strong northeastern wind caught and drove the ship. The men managed with difficulty to secure the vessel, but the storm grew severe and overpowered them. They threw the cargo overboard to lighten the ship. Unfortunately, those measures did little to assuage the rough seas. The crew felt that all was lost (v. 20).

Now remember, this was ancient shipping. They charted their path by the position of the stars. If the weather grew stormy or overcast, a vessel could easily become lost.

By verse 27 the ship was hopelessly drifting. In verse 41 it ran aground. The waves were so rough that they began to break apart the stern. That is when the centurion ordered everyone to abandon ship.

In the midst of the storm, Paul stood full of hope and salvation. He said, "I believe in God." What a picture of faith!

What is striking about Paul is that he did not despair. Like the Moravian Christians on Wesley's ship, Paul was prepared to

die. In fact, he looked forward to death as a reunion with the
Lord. Yet Paul knew that death would not touch him on that
voyage. So he got on with life and with God's purposes. He
knew that God was real. As the Lord of all nature, He could use a
storm for His ends.

Often a storm will sharpen our vision and cause us to see
what is really important. In the storm, the crew threw out its
unnecessary cargo. Storms cause people to let go of life's apparent securities. Either they leave us adrift to ourselves, or they
cause us to cling to the Rock of Ages. Paul understood that well.
He learned to lay aside every weight in his life that might keep
him from Christ.

Paul trusted God in the storm. His words echo Jesus' words
to His disciples as He walked on the sea. Jesus said, "Take courage, it is I; do not be afraid" (Matthew 14:27). No doubt Paul had
heard about the other occasion when the disciples woke Jesus
up in the storm saying, "Save us Lord; we are perishing!" Jesus
then called them "men of little faith." He rebuked them for their
timidity, for not believing in God during the storm, for being
sunny-day Christians. His disciples then marveled, saying, "What
kind of man is this, that even the winds and the sea obey Him?"
(Matthew 8:25-27).

Paul believed in Jesus. And he believed in the "God and
Father of our Lord Jesus Christ." God was sovereign over the
storm. He could stop the storm, or bring men through it.

How do you handle the storms of life? What do you do with
the contrary winds? What happens to you in shipwrecks? Paul
believed in God, despite the circumstances imposed by life.

THE CIRCUMSTANCES IMPOSED BY GOD

One more set of circumstances tells us about Paul's faith:
the circumstances imposed by God. Do not misconstrue this to
suggest that God's providence does not extend to men and nature. Of course it does, and Paul would be the first to admit it.
However, in our text, God spoke to Paul personally and revealed
to Paul His sovereign will. That is certainly a unique circumstance in our chapter.

Paul believed in God's sovereignty. He was encouraged when the angel appeared and told him he must go to Rome. He said that in spite of how things appeared, "you must stand before Caesar; and behold, God has granted you all those who are sailing with you" (v. 24).

Paul's belief in God's sovereignty did not make him irresponsible. The sovereignty of God and the responsibility of man are twin themes in Paul's life. They are evident everywhere in Acts.

During his trial we saw that Paul appealed to Caesar to avoid being sent to Jerusalem. Nevertheless, God told Paul that he would go to Rome. Now in chapter 27, Paul is reassured that God's sovereign plan will be carried out. Did he then sit back and wait for God to act? No, he was faithful and acted responsibly. Paul warned the centurion of the dangers of sailing in winter. With the others, Paul prayed for day to come. When some attempted to escape, he said, "Unless these men remain in the ship, you yourselves cannot be saved" (v. 31). How could Paul say that when earlier he had said, "There shall be no loss of life among you, but only of the ship" (v. 22)? And why did Paul exhort the men to eat for strength if they would be saved?

The answer is that Paul believed in the gospel mystery with all his life. He affirmed that God was in control, accomplishing His will. Yet he understood that we must do the work of the Lord.

Like Paul, Christians are to obey and act in good conscience. Passivity is out. However, affirming God's sovereignty brings significance to our own actions. Many of the great Christians in history have tenaciously held to both truths. We must do the same as we encounter the storms of life.

Paul made his great confession in every kind of circumstance imaginable. His faith in the Lord freed him from circumstances imposed by men. It emboldened him to the circumstances imposed by life itself. It made him responsible in the circumstances ordained by his sovereign Lord.

Paul's belief in God was the central feature of his life. He knew that if God was not Lord *of* all, he was not Lord *at all*.

What kind of confession do you make on a stormy day?

Hebrews 11-12 tell us of the great Old Testament heros of faith. That catalog ends with these words: "Therefore, since we have so great a cloud of witnesses surrounding us, let us also lay aside every encumbrance and sin which so easily entangles us, and let us run with endurance the race that is set before us, fixing our eyes on Jesus, the author and perfecter of faith" (Hebrews 12:1-2).

Remember

The way we endure a crisis tells a lot about our faith. It indicates whether faith is a vital reliance on God or a fair-weather adornment.

Christ's reign in the heart transforms a captive man so that no circumstance tyrannizes him.

Often a storm will sharpen our vision so that we see what is really important.

Paul knew that if God was not Lord of all, He was not Lord at all.

Questions

1. What was Paul's reaction in the midst of circumstances imposed by others?
2. How is life often like Paul's storm?
3. Why did Paul not despair in the storm?
4. What is the relationship between God's sovereignty and man's responsibility?

Assignment

Make a comparison between Paul's experience and those encountered by Joseph in the Old Testament. Discover specific examples of how Joseph dealt with the types of circumstances we studied in Paul's life.

Acts 28
Luke's Final Report

The Spirit of Christ is the spirit of missions, and the nearer we get to Him the more intensely missionary we must become.

— Henry Martyn

Paul longed to visit Rome—not to do business, not as a tourist, but as an apostle of Jesus Christ. Three years earlier he had written an important letter to the Roman church. Now he would visit his Christian brothers face-to-face. He would preach in the corridors of ancient imperial Rome. He would take his appeal before Caesar himself.

Luke wrote two records for his friend Theophilus. The first book we recognize as the gospel of Luke. It describes all that Jesus did and taught. The second book we call the Acts of the Apostles. It describes all that the apostles did and taught.

Acts 28 is the final section of Luke's two-volume contribution to the multi-volume history of the Christian church. At the end of Luke's account, one senses that there remains more to be written. Underneath the final paragraph of chapter 28, we expect the words "The Beginning." For it is certainly not the end of the acts of God but only of Luke's report.

Many of the apostolic acts went unrecorded. In the providence of God, those have been kept from us. Likewise, there were many other acts of God. For God was creating a new people—a church—composed of men from every race and nation.

Luke's theological history of the church was specially inspired for the cannon of Scripture. We look to his account as a model by which we measure our own churches. It proclaims the same Lord, the same Spirit, and the same gospel that we proclaim. In the twentieth century, we are still contributing sequel manuscripts for the history of the church of Christ.

As we add our own pages to that historical record, it becomes important to know how the canonical book of Acts ends. What was taking place in Acts 28? What situation are we left with? What was Paul doing in Rome?

Luke's final report provides us with the answers. There are four areas of interest that Luke presents in chapter 28.

PAUL'S PROGRESS IN ROME

In Acts 1, the original apostles received the commission to go into all the world and be witnesses. Paul was not a charter member of that group. His apostolic calling came in a special encounter with the risen Christ on the Damascus road. But despite Paul's late calling, he was faithful just the same. While others wanted to tie the gospel to Jerusalem, Paul brought the message to Asia Minor, Achaia, and Macedonia. He was a faithful witness. He lived up to the call of Jesus Christ.

In verse 14 we find the relieving words "and thus we came to Rome." If you have followed Paul's journey and trail closely, you sense that Paul and his companions were relieved to arrive. At last, his trial would come to an end. Safety and release seemed probable. At last, his desire to be with those Christian brothers and sisters would be realized.

The long journey had taken its toll on Paul. In fact, chapter 28 begins with Paul and his shipwrecked companions swimming to the shore of Malta. Then after three months, they sailed for Syracuse, then Rhegium, and on to Puteoli. Finally, from Puteoli they traveled by land to Rome. God had assured Paul that he would preach in Rome. He had been promised safety. In Acts 28 we see that all of those promises were fulfilled.

The end of Acts 28 has long puzzled Bible students. The chapter closes with Paul involved in energetic ministry. The final verses read, "And he stayed two full years in his own rented quarters, and was welcoming all who came to him, preaching the kingdom of God, and teaching concerning the Lord Jesus Christ with all openness, unhindered."

On that optimistic note, the book of Acts closes. The reader is left hanging.

Paul came to Rome in A.D. 60. He was beheaded there between 64 and 68. Scholars disagree on two points: the exact date of his death and Paul's activities between A.D. 62 and his execution.

In Romans 15:28 Paul writes that he hopes to pass through Rome on his way to Spain. And Luke implies in Acts 28:30 that, after two years of house arrest in Rome, things changed for Paul.

There are three possibilities offered to explain what changed. Some think that Paul was found guilty and then executed around A.D. 64. Others think he was found innocent, then freed to travel to Spain. Upon returning to Rome, he was rearrested and put to death. Still others think Paul was banished to Spain and executed when he returned to Rome to defend Christians during Nero's persecution.

Exactly what happened, we do not know. All we can be sure of are those two years of imprisonment between A.D. 60-62. What do they tell us about Paul?

Paul was encouraged upon meeting his fellow Christians as he approached Rome. No doubt it was a grand union and reunion. They enjoyed rich fellowship together. Paul's epistle to the Romans tells us who some of his Roman friends were. There was Phoebe, a friend Paul knew from the church at Cenchrea. There were Prisca and Aquila, tentmakers from Corinth. There was Epaenetus whom Paul calls, "my beloved . . . the first convert to Christ from Asia" (Romans 16:5). Others there Paul referred to as "fellow workers" and "kinsmen." Those were dear friends.

In Romans 1:15, Paul says he is eager to preach the gospel to them. Therefore, we can be assured that Paul built up the saints in Rome. His epistle to the Romans is so rich that he probably expounded its contents for them, drawing out its implications and applications. What an exposition that must have been!

Then also, Paul met with the local Jewish leaders. He was not afraid of those who disagreed with him. He invited them over for friendly debates. They came in great numbers. Once they settled down, Paul "was explaining to them by solemnly testifying about the kingdom of God, and trying to persuade them concerning Jesus . . . from morning until evening" (v. 23).

Right to the end of his life, Paul proclaimed Christ. Day in and day out, he was expounding and testifying and preaching and teaching. He was carrying out his commission as an apostle. He was going strong as Jesus' disciple. Luke does not end his account with a dead apostle, or a despondent apostle. Rather, he pictures Paul as we should remember him—intensively active for Christ. What a superb model Luke upholds for us today!

<h3 style="text-align:center">The Recipients of the Gospel</h3>

In chapter 28 Luke also shows an interest in the recipient of Paul's message.

The emphasis is not on the Roman Christians. Luke reports that Paul's first major effort was to reach the Jews. In verses 17-20, Paul explains his case to them, defending his own innocence. In verses 21-22, we hear their initial reaction. They were wary of Christians—a "sect," they say, that is "spoken against everywhere." They knew nothing of Paul's case, and they wanted to hear his views.

After Paul's major effort to convince them that Jesus was the Christ, we read of their characteristic response. Verse 24 says that some were convinced, whereas others disbelieved. Unfortunately, Luke gives no evidence that those who were convinced personally accepted the message. The final reaction of the Jews was to depart from Paul debating among themselves.

Before they left, however, Paul gave them one last thought. He quoted Isaiah 6 and pronounced the fact that their hearts had been hardened, just like their fathers'. In essence Paul said, "Like father, like son." Isaiah said that regardless of what those people saw or heard, they were blind and deaf to the Word of God.

Is that a final rejection of the Jews? I think not. Paul elsewhere expressed his hope that his own people would embrace the gospel (Romans 11:25-32). In his missionary work, he faithfully maintained the priority of going to the Jews first. Acts 1:8 speaks of being a witness in Jerusalem, Judea, and Samaria, and then to the ends of the earth. Paul had gone to the Jews in dispersion. Only after they clearly rejected his message did he turn to the Gentiles.

Acts 28 is significant in that respect: Paul has now turned fully to the Gentiles. The Gentile was the new recipient of the gospel. Paul said to the Jews, "Let it be known to you therefore, that this salvation of God has been sent to the Gentiles; they will also listen!" (v. 28).

Paul's turning points the way to a definite Gentile mission. It was the Gentiles in Rome who apparently accepted Paul's message. That is why the word *all* in verse 30 is so important. Paul "welcomed all who came to him."

THE MESSAGE OF PAUL

There is a third area of interest for Luke in chapter 28, the message of Paul. Luke repeats the content of Paul's message twice. We find it in verses 23-31. Paul preached the kingdom of God and taught that Jesus was the Christ. The rule of God was the rule of God's agent. That agent was the Messiah. The Messiah was Jesus. Paul believed that the gospel of Christ was the fulfillment of Israel's religion. All of Old Testament history pointed to Jesus. Paul set out to prove his point from Scripture.

That has been the message of the church right from the beginning. In Acts 1:3, Luke reminds us that Jesus spoke to the disciples about the kingdom of God. In Acts 2:36, Peter preaches at Pentecost that Jesus is "both Lord and Christ." In Acts 8:12, Philip preaches "the good news about the kingdom of God and the name of Jesus Christ." In Acts 20:21 and 25, Paul bids farewell to the Ephesian elders, telling them that he has faithfully declared the Lord Jesus Christ and preached the kingdom. Paul preached what he had received from the beginning. He passed on the deposit of faith.

By Acts 28, the gospel had passed through at least three different cultures: the Hebrew environment of Jerusalem, the Greek environment of Achaia and Asia Minor, and now the Latin culture of Rome. Though Paul tried to be all things to all people, and though he used the thought forms of each culture, he preached a basic gospel that was always the same. And he preached it from the Scriptures.

The gospel for the twentieth and twenty-first centuries need not be abridged or transformed or "demythologized." Yes, we must communicate in words that can be understood by modern man, but we dare not alter the message. Paul preached the old, old story. So must we. He spoke, says verse 28, of "the salvation of God." He assumed that Hebrews, Greeks, and Latins needed saving.

The Hebrews, with all their great religious traditions, needed God's grace. The Greeks, with all their intricate philosophies, needed God's wisdom. The Latins, with all their civilized Roman roads and laws, needed God's way to heaven and God's gospel as a road map.

So it is with men today. Modern, sophisticated, urban men need saving, and it is only a supernatural God who can get them out of the mess they are in.

Of course, at the end of his life Paul's understanding of his message was more profound than at first. But it was, in essence, the same gospel of our Lord Jesus Christ.

THE MISSION OF THE CHURCH

Finally, we must conclude by looking at Luke's interest in the mission of the church. For Luke, it is a mission yet to be accomplished. He leaves his account in chapter 28 open-ended.

In Acts 1, the disciples were instructed by Jesus to wait in Jerusalem until they were told what to do. They knew there was much work to be done, because their mission was to be worldwide. But in Acts 1, they had not yet received their marching orders from the Holy Spirit.

In Acts 28, we find that a gospel beachhead had been established in Rome. The mission had moved beyond Jewish populations. But Rome was not the ends of the earth. If anything, it was considered the center. In those days, "the ends of the earth" meant the ends of the earth as it was known. Spain was as far west as one could go. The Romans had conquered southern Britain in A.D. 43. Shortly before that time they had ventured into northern Germanic lands. But no one knew what lay beyond those regions.

By A.D. 60, when Paul arrived in Rome, the gospel had not yet reached the ends of the known world. For Luke, Paul, and Christians of the day, there was a great task before them.

Compared to that time, our understanding of the world is drastically different. Today we find approximately 223 states and territories in the world. There are about 5,770 different languages spoken. Every year around 121 million people are born. Of the world, approximately 23 percent is nominally Christian. Much of the world is officially atheist; some animist; some Buddhist; some Islamic.

It is a good thing that Luke's history in Acts is open-ended. In his own day, the mission was just beginning. In our day, 1,900 years later, we can look back on great advances, but the task before us is enormous.

What will your part be in this great missionary endeavor? This "salvation of God," Paul says, has been sent to the Gentiles—"they will listen!"

The final volumes of the succession of the gospel have yet to be written. The Acts of the apostles are complete. But the acts of the disciples are still getting under way. And the acts of God have never ceased.

How are you acting as a disciple? And how is God acting through you? By God's grace, let us follow Paul's example and keep going strong in the task of world evangelization yet before us.

Remember

To the end of his life, Paul proclaimed Christ.

Paul had gone to the Jews in dispersion. Only after they clearly rejected his message did he turn to the Gentiles.

Though Paul tried to be all things to all people, and though he used the thought forms of each culture, he preached a basic gospel that was always the same. And he preached it from the Scriptures.

The final volumes of the succession of the gospel have yet to be written.

Questions

1. Why was Paul so interested in preaching in Rome?
2. Describe the type of work Paul engaged in during his time in Rome.
3. Capsulize the message of Paul according to Luke's account in Acts 28.
4. How does the church of today fit into the book of Acts?

Assignment

Consult various commentaries to find out how they approach Paul's years in Rome. List various options and the reasons given. Which do you find most likely and why?

Appendix 1
Prayer

I. References to Prayer
1:14, 24; 2:42; 3:1; 4:24-30; 6:4, 6; 8:15, 22, 24; 9:11; 10:2-4; 10:30-31; 11:5; 12:5, 12; 13:3; 14:23; 16:13, 16, 25; 20:5, 36; 21:5; 22:17; 27:35; 28:8

II. Centrality of Prayer
   A. Key discipline, 2:42
   B. Choosing an apostle, 1:24
   C. Apostolic duty, 6:4
   D. Apostolic ministry, 14:23

III. Situations of Prayer
   A. Confident witness, 4:24-30
   B. Receiving the Spirit, 8:14-17
   C. Forgiveness, 8:22
   D. Intercession, 8:24; 12:5, 12
   E. Praise, 4:24
   F. Healing, 4:30; 9:40; 28:8
   G. Mission, 13:3
   H. Emergency, 12:5
   I. Farewell, 20:36; 21:5
   J. Mealtime, 27:35
   K. Decisions, 1:24
   L. Direction, 1:14; 9:11
   M. Captivity, 16:25

IV. Methods of Prayer
   A. Individual, 9:11
   B. Corporate, 12:12
   C. With fasting, 13:3; 14:23
   D. With laying of hands, 6:6; 13:3

    E. With Scripture, 4:24-26

    F. With unity, 1:14

    G. Hours of prayer, 3:1; 10:3, 9

    H. Continual prayer, 1:14; 2:42; 10:2

    I. With hymns of praise, 16:25

  V. Place of Prayer

    A. Upper room, 1:13-14

    B. Bedside, 9:40

    C. Housetop, 10:9

    D. Home, 12:12

    E. Prison, 16:25

    F. Beach, 21:5

    G. Temple, 22:17

    H. Storm at sea, 27:35

 VI. Actual Prayers

    A. 1:24-25

    B. 4:24-30

VII. Answers to Prayer

    A. They receive boldness, 4:31

    B. They receive the Holy Spirit, 8:16-17

    C. Dead women raised, 9:40-41

    D. Gospel comes to Cornelius, 10:4, 31

    E. Angel releases Peter, 12:5-7

    F. Successful missionary journey, 13:3

    G. Sick man healed, 28:8-9

VIII. People of Prayer

    A. Gathered church, 1:14

    B. Disciples, 3:1

    C. Apostles, 6:4

    D. Simon the magician, 8:9-24

    E. Non-Christian centurion, 10:2

    F. Saul the persecutor, 9:11

    G. Elders, 20:36

Appendix 2
The Holy Spirit

I. References to the Spirit
   1:2, 5, 8, 16; 2:3-4, 17-18, 33, 38-39; 4:8, 25, 31; 5:3, 9, 32; 6:3, 5, 10; 7:51, 55; 8:15, 17-19, 29, 39; 9:17, 31; 10:19, 38, 45, 47; 11:12, 15-16, 24, 28; 12:7; 13:2, 4, 9, 52; 15:8, 28; 16:6-7; 19:2, 6; 20:23, 28; 21:4, 11; 23:8-9; 28:25

II. Recipients of the Spirit
   A. Disciples, 1:8; 2:3
   B. All mankind, 2:17
   C. Those far off (us), 2:39
   D. Jesus, 1:2
   E. Peter, 4:8
   F. Servant/deacons, 6:3
   G. Stephen, 6:5, 10; 7:55
   H. Ananias and Paul, 9:17; 13:9
   I. Church, 9:31
   J. Gentiles, 10:45; 11:15; 15:8
   K. Barnabas, 11:24
   L. Agabus, 11:28

III. Names of the Spirit
   A. Spirit of the Lord, 5:9
   B. Holy Spirit, many references
   C. Spirit, 2:17
   D. Spirit of, 16:7

IV. Revelation and the Spirit
   A. David, 1:16; 4:25
   B. Isaiah, 28:25

V. Nature of the Spirit
  A. Promised by the Father, 2:33
  B. Given by the Father, 5:32
  C. Poured forth by the Son, 2:33
  D. A gift, 2:38; 10:45
  E. Active in Jesus, 1:2; 10:38

VI. Work of the Spirit
  A. Came upon, 1:8; 19:6; 10:44
  B. Filled, 4:8; 6:3, 5; 7:55; 9:17; 13:9
  C. Bestowed, 8:18
  D. Received, 2:38; 8:15, 17; 19:2
  E. Poured, 2:17, 33; 10:45
  F. Resting on, 2:3
  G. Solemnly testifies, 20:23
  H. Baptizes, 1:5
  I. Comforts, 9:31
  J. Empowers, 1:8
  K. Directs, 8:29, 39; 10:19; 11:12; 15:28; 16:6-7
  L. Sets apart, 13:2
  M. Sends, 13:4
  N. Appoints, 20:28

VII. Means of receiving the Spirit
  A. Prayer, 4:31; 8:15
  B. Repentance and baptism, 2:38
  C. Before baptism, 10:47
  D. Fasting and worship, 13:2
  E. Laying of hands, 8:17; 19:6

VIII. Manifestation of the Spirit
  A. Winds, 2:2
  B. Tongues, 2:3-4; 19:6
  C. Joy, 2:13
  D. Prophecy, 2:12; 11:28; 19:6; 21:11
  E. Boldness, 4:31

IX. Opposition to the Spirit
  A. Lie against, 5:3
  B. Put to test, 5:9
  C. Resist, 7:51
  D. Deny, 21:11

Appendix 3
The Church

I. Roles in the Church
  A. Apostle
      1. Commissioned by Jesus, 1:2
      2. Witness to the resurrection, 1:22
      3. A ministry, 1:25
      4. Centrality of apostolic teaching, 2:42
      5. Signs and wonders, 2:43
      6. In charge of distribution, 4:35
      7. Commission a committee of servants, 6:5-6
      8. Bestow Spirit, 8:18
      9. Applied to more than the original twelve, 14:14
      10. Applied to the original twelve, 1:25
      11. Authority of apostles, 15:23
      12. Ruled the church with elders, 16:4
      13. Summon congregation, 6:2
      14. Primacy of apostolic preaching, 6:2
  B. Elder
      1. Parallel of elders in synagogue and temple, 4:5; 22:5; 23:14; 24:1
      2. Relief appropriate/supplies, 11:30
      3. Appointed in every church, 14:23
      4. Lead church to Jerusalem with apostles, 4:6; 15:2
      5. Lead church of Ephesus, 20:17
      6. An overseer, 20:28

   C. Prophet
      1. Shared between churches, 11:27
      2. Lead Antioch church along with the teachers and Saul, 13:1
      3. Encourage with a message, 15:32
      4. Prophetesses, 21:9
      5. Foretelling, 21:11
   D. Deacon
      1. Committee to serve tables, 6:3 (not technically an office at this stage)
   E. Evangelist
      1. Philip, 21:8
      2. The apostles (though not explicitly stated)
   F. Priests
      1. Becoming obedient to the faith, 6:7
   G. Congregation
      1. Summoned by the apostles, 6:2; 15:30
      2. Give approval to apostolic decision, 6:5
      3. Choose people to care for widows, 6:5
 II. Development of offices
   A. Jerusalem church
      1. Apostles and elders, 15:2
      2. Prophets, 11:27
      3. Committee of servants, 6:3
   B. Antioch church
      1. Apostles, prophets, and teachers, 13:1
      2. Probably elders, 14:23
   C. Elsewhere
      1. Apostles and elders, 14:23
III. Primacy
   A. Jerusalem
      1. Call a council, 15:2
      2. Deliver its decrees, 15:30; 16:4
   B. Antioch
      1. Missionary center, chapters 13-21

IV. Church organization
   A. Intern/assistant, 12:25
   B. Conference/council, 15:1-35
   C. Committee, 6:3
   D. Reports, 15:30; 16:4
   E. Commissioning, 6:6; 13:3; 14:23
   F. Decision making
      1. Early on, apostles summon congregation, 6:1-7
      2. Later on, apostles appoint elders who oversee congregations, 20:17-38

V. Church Life
   A. Teaching
      1. Based on apostolic preaching, 2:42
      2. In the Temple, 5:42
      3. In the home, 5:42; 20:20
      4. Publicly, 20:20
      5. Scope—the whole purpose of God, 20:27
   B. Fellowship
      1. Importance of, 2:42
      2. Meals together, 2:46
      3. Common goals, 4:32
      4. Giving, 2:44-45; 4:34
      5. Between churches, 11:29
   C. Lord's Supper
      1. Continually, 2:42
      2. House to house, 2:46
      3. On first day of week, 20:7
   D. Prayer
      1. Centrality, 2:42
      2. See Appendix 1: Prayer
   E. Baptism
      1. Belief and Spirit indwelling, 8:16; 10:47; 19:2
      2. Meaning
         a) Repentance and belief, 19:4
         b) Forgiveness, 2:38
         c) A wash, 22:16
      3. Re-baptism, 19:3-5
      4. Household baptism, 16:15, 33
      5. Method, 8:38

  F. Other disciplines
   1. Vows, 18:18
   2. Lord's Day, 20:7; 13:14; 17:2; 18:4
   3. Feasts, chapter 2; 20:16
   4. Temple attendance, 2:46
   5. Synagogue attendance, 9:20; 18:26; 22:19
   6. Giving, 4:34
   7. Worship and fasting, 13:2

VI. Church and Home
 A. Salvation and the home, 11:14; 16:31-34; 18:8
 B. Met in homes, 8:3
 C. Teaching and preaching in homes, 5:42; 20:20
 D. Breaking bread in homes, 2:46
 E. Selling homes, 4:34

VII. Problems
 A. Persecution, 4:3; 5:18; 7:59; 9:1; 12:1
 B. Famine and poverty, 11:28-29
 C. False teaching, 20:29-31
 D. Disagreement, 15:2, 39
 E. Discrimination, 6:1
 F. Lying, 5:1-11

VIII. Name of Church Members
 A. The congregation, 4:32
 B. The congregation of disciples, 6:2
 C. The disciples, 9:26
 D. The Way, 9:2
 E. The saints, 9:13
 F. Christians, 11:26
 G. Brethren, 11:29
 H. The church (at Jerusalem, Antioch, and so on), 11:22; 13:1
 I. The church of God, 20:28
 J. The flock, 20:28

IX. Church Mission (see Appendix 4: Missions)

Appendix 4
Missions

I. Commission
  A. By Jesus, 1:8
  B. By God, 13:47
  C. By an angel, 5:20
  D. By church leaders, 13:3
II. Overview of Missions
  A. Commission, chapter 1
  B. Empowering, chapter 2
  C. Scattering, chapter 8
  D. Conversion of Saul, chapter 9
  E. Mission in Palestine, chapters 10-12
  F. First missionary journey, chapters 13-14
  G. Second missionary journey, chapters 16-18
  H. Third missionary journey, chapters 18-21
  I. Paul's mission to Rome, chapters 21-28
III. Mission fields
  A. Jerusalem, Judea, Samaria, 1:8
  B. Temple, 5:20
  C. Villages, 8:25
  D. Whole island, 13:6
  E. Synagogue, 13:5
  F. Gentiles, 13:47
  G. Macedonia, 16:9-10
  H. Marketplace, 17:17
  I. Areopagus, 17:19
  J. Ends of the earth, 1:8; 13:47

IV. Doctrine of Missions
   A. Witness to resurrection, 1:22; 2:32; 3:15
   B. Spoke in His name, 4:17; 8:12
   C. Spoke of what they saw and heard, 4:20
   D. Repentance and the forgiveness of sins, 5:31
   E. Preaching Jesus as Christ, 8:5; 18:5; 28:31
   F. Preaching the kingdom of God, 8:12; 19:8; 28:31
   G. The good news of the promise, 13:32
   H. Salvation under no other name, 4:12

V. Call of Missions
   A. Repent and be baptized in the name of Jesus, 2:38
   B. Repent and return, 3:19
   C. Everyone who believes in Him receives forgiveness of sins, 10:43
   D. Turn from the vain things of this world, 14:15
   E. Believe on the Lord Jesus Christ and thou shalt be saved, 16:31

VI. Words of Missions
   A. Witness, 1:8
   B. Giving witness, 4:33
   C. Preaching, 8:12
   D. Proclaim, 8:5
   E. Make disciples, 14:21
   F. Reasoned, 18:4
   G. Persuade, 19:8

VII. The Spirit and Missions
   A. Sets apart, 13:2
   B. Sends, 13:4
   C. Directs, 16:6-7

VIII. Positive Response to Missions
   A. Received the word, 2:41
   B. Being saved, 2:47
   C. Believed, 4:4
   D. Obedient to the faith, 6:7
   E. Turned to the Lord, 9:35; 11:21

Appendix 5
The Word of God

I. Written Word (Old Testament Scripture)
   A. Direct quotations
      1. Chapter 1 (Psalms 69, 109)
      2. Chapter 2 (Psalms 16, 89, 110, 132; Joel 2; 2 Samuel 7)
      3. Chapter 3 (Genesis 22; Deuteronomy 18)
      4. Chapter 4 (Exodus 20; Psalms 2, 118)
      5. Chapter 7 (Genesis 12, 15, 17; Exodus 1-3, 32; Deuteronomy 18; Amos 5; Isaiah 66)
      6. Chapter 8 (Isaiah 53)
      7. Chapter 13 (1 Samuel 13; Psalms 2, 16; Isaiah 55; Habakkuk 1; Isaiah 49)
      8. Chapter 14 (Exodus 20)
      9. Chapter 15 (Amos 9)
      10. Chapter 23 (Exodus 22)
      11. Chapter 28 (Isaiah 6)
   B. Scripture and Fulfillment
      1. Messianic, 3:24; 4:25-26; 13:22-23; 26:22
      2. Judas, 1:16
      3. Pilate, 13:28
   C. Scripture and the Holy Spirit
      1. The Spirit foretells, 1:16
      2. The Spirit speaks rightly, 28:25
      3. The Spirit speaks through men
         a) David, 1:16; 4:25
         b) Isaiah, 28:25

D. Use of Scripture
   1. Apologetic, 18:28
   2. To test preaching, 17:11
   3. Worship, 13:15
   4. Teaching, 18:24-25
II. Preached Word
   A. Names of the word
      1. The word of the Lord, 13:49
      2. The word, 4:4
      3. The word of God, 4:31
      4. The word of this salvation, 13:26
      5. The word of His grace, 14:3; 20:32
      6. The word of the gospel, 15:7
      7. The gospel of the grace of God, 20:24
      8. The apostle's teaching, 2:42
      9. The message of this life, 5:20
      10. The good news, 8:12
   B. Goal of preaching
      1. Receiving the word, 2:41; 17:11
      2. Believing the word, 4:4; 15:7
      3. Rejoicing and glorifying the word of the Lord, 13:48
      4. Building up and giving an inheritance, 20:32
   C. Method of preaching
      1. With confidence, 4:29
      2. With boldness, 4:31
      3. With comprehensiveness, 20:27
   D. Centrality of preaching
      1. The doctrine of the church, 2:42
      2. The main duty of an apostle, 6:2
      3. To be coupled with prayer, 6:4
      4. A ministry that is received, 20:24
   E. Power of preaching
      1. Kept on spreading, 6:7
      2. Continued to grow and be multiplied, 12:24
      3. Growing mightily and prevailing, 19:20
   F. Content of preaching
      1. Peace through Jesus Christ, the Lord of all, 10:36

G. Test of preaching
1. The written Word, 17:11
H. Sermons
1. Peter
   a) At Pentecost, 2:14-40
   b) At the Temple, 3:12-26
   c) Before the high priest, 4:8-12
   d) At Cornelius's house, 10:34-48
2. Stephen
   a) At stoning, 7:1-53
3. Philip
   a) With the eunuch, 8:35-37
4. Paul
   a) At Antioch of Pisidia, 13:16-41
   b) At Lystra, 14:15-17
   c) At Philippi, 16:30-32
   d) At Athens, 17:22-31
   e) At Miletus, 20:18-35 (to Christians)
   f) At Jerusalem, 22:1-21; 23:1-6
   g) At Caesarea, 24:10-21; 26:1-29

Appendix 6
Jesus Christ

I. Titles
   A. Lord, 1:6
   B. Lord Jesus, 1:21
   C. The Christ, 2:31
   D. Lord and Christ, 2:36
   E. Jesus Christ the Nazarene, 3:6
   F. Jesus Christ, 3:6
   G. Servant, 3:13
   H. The Holy and Righteous One, 3:14
   I. The Prince of life, 3:15
   J. The cornerstone, 4:11
   K. Thy holy servant Jesus, 4:27
   L. A Prince and Savior, 5:31
   M. The Righteous One, 7:52
   N. The Son of Man, 7:56
   O. Son of God, 9:20
   P. Lord of all, 10:36
   Q. Lord Jesus Christ, 15:26
   R. Thy Holy One, 13:35

II. Humanity
   A. Mother and brothers, 1:14
   B. The Nazarene, 2:22
   C. A man, 2:22
   D. Was crucified, 2:36; 10:39
   E. Put to death, 2:23; 8:33; 10:39
   F. He suffered 1:3; 3:18; 17:3; 26:23
   G. Was rejected, 4:11
   H. Teacher of the kingdom, 1:1-4

III. Deity
   A. Miracles
      1. Attested by God with miracles, 2:22
      2. His name heals, 4:10
      3. Jesus heals through the apostles, 9:34
      4. Exorcism in His name, 16:18; 19:13-16
   B. Relationship with the Father and the Spirit
      1. Exalted to God's right hand, 2:33; 5:31; 7:55
      2. Made Lord and Christ, 2:36
      3. God foretold His suffering, 3:18
      4. God raised Him, 2:32
      5. God gave Him the promise of the Holy Spirit, 2:33
      6. Son of God, 9:20
      7. God anointed Him with the Holy Spirit and power, 10:38
      8. God was with Him, 10:38
      9. God fulfilled His promise in Christ's resurrection, 13:33
   C. Death
      1. Overcame death, 2:24
      2. Undergoes no decay, 2:27
      3. The church is obtained by His blood, 20:28
      4. Grants forgiveness, 13:38
      5. Christ had to suffer and raise, 17:3
      6. Impossible for death to hold Him, 2:24
      7. Delivered up according to God's plan, 2:23
   D. Resurrection
      1. God raised Him, 2:24; 3:15; 4:10; 13:33-37
      2. Witnesses of the resurrection, 1:3; 3:15

E. Present work
   1. Exalted, 2:33; 5:31; 7:55
   2. Ascended, 1:9-11
   3. Receives spirits of those who die in Him, 7:59
   4. Directs, 16:7
   5. Gives ministries, 20:24
F. Future
   1. Will come as He left, 1:11
   2. God appointed Him as judge, 10:42
   3. Will restore kingdom, 1:6

Appendix 7
Salvation

I. The Call of Salvation
   A. All men everywhere should repent, 17:30
II. The Grace of Salvation
   A. Controversy over works righteousness, 15:1
   B. Saved by grace, 15:11
   C. Those who were appointed believed, 13:48
   D. Those who received grace believed, 18:27
   E. The promise is for those whom God calls, 2:39
   F. God grants repentance to the Gentiles, 11:18
   G. The Lord opens hearts, 16:14
III. The Name of Salvation
   A. Whoever calls upon the name of the Lord shall be saved, 2:21
   B. Baptism in the name of Jesus, 2:38
   C. Faith is in His name, 3:16
   D. No other name by which men are saved, 4:12
   E. Forgiveness in His name, 10:43
IV. The Benefits of Salvation
   A. Forgiveness of sins, 2:38; 5:31; 10:43; 13:38
   B. The Holy Spirit, 2:38
   C. Strength and health, 3:16
   D. Life, 11:18
   E. Eternal life, 13:48
   F. Freedom, 13:39

V. The Response to Salvation
  A. Repentance
    1. Repent and return to God, 3:19; 26:20
    2. Jesus grants repentance and forgiveness, 5:31
    3. Repent of wickedness, 8:22
    4. Repentance leads to life, 11:18
    5. Men everywhere should repent, 17:30
    6. Do deeds appropriate to repentance, 26:20
  B. Faith
    1. Believe on Him for forgiveness of sins, 10:43
    2. Faith in His name, 3:16
    3. Many who believed turned to the Lord, 11:21
    4. Believe in the Lord Jesus Christ, 16:31
    5. Everyone who believes is freed, 13:39
  C. Baptism
    1. Baptism and washing away of sins, 22:16
    2. They received the word and were baptized, 2:41
    3. Baptize in the name of Jesus Christ, 10:48
    4. John's baptism, 19:4
    5. Household baptism, 16:33
  D. Combination
    1. Repent and be baptized in the name of Jesus Christ, 2:38
    2. Be saved from this perverse generation, 2:40
    3. Turn from vain things to a living God, 14:15
    4. Believe and be baptized, 18:8
    5. Testifying repentance and faith, 20:21

Appendix 8
Approximate Chronology I

Emperors	Kings			
Caesar Augustus 30 B.C.-A.D. 14	Herod the Great 37-4 B.C.			
	Archelaus 4 B.C.-A.D. 6 ethnarch Judea Samaria Idumea	Herod Antipas 4 B.C.-A.D. 39 tetrarch Galilee Perea	Herod Philip 4 B.C.-A.D. 34 tetrarch Ituraea Trachonitis Gaulanitis Auranitis Batanea	Coponius A.D. 6-10
				M. Ambivius A.D. 10-13
Tiberius Caesar A.D. 14-37				Annius Rufus A.D. 13-15
				Valerius Gratus A.D. 15-26
				Pontius Pilate A.D. 26-36
Caligula A.D. 37-41				Marcellus A.D. 36-38
Claudius A.D. 41-54	Herod Agrippa I King of Judea A.D. 41-44			Cuspius Fadus A.D. 44-46
				Tiberius Alexander A.D. 46-48
	Herod Agrippa II A.D. 48-70 tetrarch Galilee, Perea,			Ventidius Cumanus A.D. 48-52

Emperors   Kings

Nero
A.D. 54-68

Northeastern
    Palestine

Antonius Felix
A.D. 52-59

Porcius Festus
A.D. 59-61

Clodius
    Albinas
A.D. 61-65

Galba/Otho/
    Vitellius
A.D. 68-6

Gessius Florus
A.D. 65-70

Vespian
    A.D. 69-79

Appendix 9
Approximate Chronology II

Event	Bible	Date
Public ministry of Jesus	Gospels/Acts	C. A.D. 27-30
Crucifixion and ascension	Gospels/Acts	A.D. 30
Pentecost/church founded	Acts 2	A.D. 30
Death of Stephen/persecution	Acts 6-8	C. A.D. 32-35
Paul's conversion	Acts 9	C. A.D. 32-35
Founding of church at Antioch	Acts 11	A.D. 41?
James, son of Zebedee, martyred	Acts 12	C. A.D. 41-43
Famine and relief fund	Acts 11	C. A.D. 45-46
First missionary journey	Acts 13-14	A.D. 46-48
Jerusalem Council	Acts 15	A.D. 48/49
Second missionary journey	Acts 15-18	A.D. 49-52
Third missionary journey	Acts 18-21	A.D. 53-57
Paul's arrest in Jerusalem	Acts 21-23	A.D. 57
Paul in Caesarea before Felix, Festus, and Agrippa	Acts 23-26	A.D. 57-59
Voyage to Rome	Acts 25-27	A.D. 59
(First) imprisonment in Rome	Acts 28	A.D. 60
Acts written		A.D. 61-63
Release		A.D. 63?
Spain		A.D. 64-67?
Second imprisonment		A.D. 67?
Nero's persecution and fire		A.D. 64
Deaths of Peter and Paul in Rome		C. A.D. 64-68
Jewish war		A.D. 66-70
Destruction of Jerusalem		A.D. 70

Appendix 10
Bibliography

Bruce, F. F. *The Acts of the Apostles: The Greek Text with Introduction and Commentary*. Grand Rapids: Eerdmans, 1951.

———. *Commentary on the Book of Acts: The English Text with Introduction, Exposition and Notes*. Vol. 5 in *The New International Commentary on the New Testament*. Grand Rapids: Eerdmans, 1954.

———. *Paul: Apostle of the Heart Set Free*. Grand Rapids: Eerdmans, 1983.

Criswell, W. A. *Acts in One Volume*. Grand Rapids: Zondervan, 1980.

Marshall, I. Howard *The Acts of the Apostles*. In *The Tyndale New Testament Commentary Series*. Grand Rapids: Eerdmans, 1980.

Morgan, G. C. *The Acts of the Apostles*. New York: Revell, 1924.

Neill, William. *The Acts of the Apostles*. In *The New Century Bible Commentary*. Grand Rapids: Eerdmans, 1973.